LEAVING CAMPUS

AND GOING TO WORK

BY

T. JASON SMITH
MHR, SPHR

ASPEN MOUNTAIN
PUBLISHING

Published by **Aspen Mountain Publishing, Sugar Hill, GA**

Discounts are available for Aspen Mountain books for quantity purchases. For details regarding bulk purchases, direct inquiries to **bulksales@aspenmtnpublishing.com** or write to us at the mailing address listed on our website **http://www.aspenmtnpublishing.com**.

Printed in the United States of America

ISBN 0-9777237-6-3

Library of Congress Control Number: 2006900089

First Edition

Thanks to...

My loving wife and best friend, **Carolyn Smith**, who has supported my dreams, no matter how extreme. Without your support, encouragement and honest feedback, this book would not have come to pass;

My friend and attorney **Julie Wallace** whose thoughtful insight and incredible penchant for detail made this a much better book than it ever could have been without her. Thank you for your candor and for reading so many drafts over so many months;

Mary Smith, Luella Mattson, and **Tom Kornegay** for their support and willingness to help me out with this project; and

Ted Kooser for his inspiration as a corporate gentleman who never relinquished his love of words. Thank you for showing that putting pen to paper, no matter what your primary vocation, is a gift that belongs to all of us.

Dedicated to...

Jaelyn Emily.
Daddy loves you.

Table of Contents

About the Author

Section 1 - Foreword

LEAVING CAMPUS

A young woman just left my office in a frame of mind I see more and more with new campus hires: a mix of confusion, borderline fatigue and a touch of disenchantment. No, I am not a doctor. I am a Human Resources Manager. I work for a corporation and I help manage the people who work here. Like a parent, I bring people into the company, help them grow, offer praise and discipline as needed, and finally watch them move on to other things as they retire or find better opportunities. It is a typical career life cycle, one that I have watched happen over and over at several different companies for the past fourteen years. The dancers change but the steps are always the same.

But seeing campus hires struggle with the same set of frustrations over and over during the first year of their first job bothers me. I am not talking about the frustration of work itself. Anyone who has ever worked at any type of job knows that type of frustration is simply unavoidable. Instead, I am talking about personal frustration that comes along in a campus hire's first year of their first real job; things like adjusting to the structure and rules of a professional job, learning to manage more money than they have ever had in a paycheck, and in some cases, even figuring out what their boss really expects them to be doing. Seeing a young professional trying to cope with so many new and different challenges at one time made me start to think, "What can I do to make a campus hire's transition to the working world a bit easier?" This book is my answer.

What is the point of this book? I simply want to give you experienced insight on topics that may help smooth your transition to the working world. Over a fourteen year career in Human Resources, I have seen many people make simple but significant mistakes early in their career. These mistakes either permanently stigmatized them in the eyes of those who controlled their careers or bruised their psyche to the point they dropped their career expectations a level as a result of their misstep. In many cases, the missteps were avoidable if someone had just spent a little time coaching them about what works and what does not work in the working world.

Who am I targeting? I am targeting students coming right off of campus who are (or will be very soon) in the first year of their first real full-time job. You know who you are: bright-eyed, eager, full of dreams, and loaded with student loans. But if you are one who has been working for a few years, I will not complain if you also take a moment to read some of the thoughts I am about to convey. Who knows? You may pick up a few ideas to help you avoid a few more bruises to your slowly toughening professional persona. The primary target, though, is the person coming straight from campus who knows little to nothing about the real world of work. I was there once and I still remember how it was.

Why am I targeting you? In many cases, employers do a relatively poor job of helping you transition from the safe, structured, and finite world of academia into the full-time working world. We basically drop you into a big pit of chaos without a clue about what you are to do next. Why? Some professionals will tell you that "if new students are put out to flounder and they survive, then we know we have a successful employee." I disagree. That is doublespeak for "If we make these new hires play a 'survival of the fittest' game, we do not have to lift a finger to help in their development and we will have a clean conscience if they fail." That is just not acceptable in my opinion. In my career, I have had no problem holding people accountable for their performance (both good and bad), but only if they had fair warning about what was expected of them and how they needed to perform to succeed. It seems only fair that you get the same courtesy, especially in your first job.

Why do I want to focus on that first year of your existence in the working world? This is one of the few times in your life when you can honestly be labeled 'high potential' because your career can only go up from where you are. You obviously invested something to get where you are right now. It may have been time. Depending on your age, your higher education could have taken at least 30% of your life to date. It may have been other opportunities. You could have been hiking the Alps or running a bar on the beach in Key West. But instead, you forewent these other opportunities to pursue your higher education. What about money? Let's not forget about money! Most of us leave school with more debt than our parents made as their first annual salary. We would not have made that investment without expecting to recover that amount plus some, correct? With all these various investments you have made, you deserve to have a fighting chance to get through your first year with a reasonable expectation of success.

From the time we are born through graduation, we live in a structured world of learning and evaluation. Everyone along the way (teachers, parents, etc.) ensures we are encapsulated in a safe world where each experience is designed to help us develop our basic knowledge (what a bird is, that hot things burn, when the sun goes down we are supposed to sleep). Part of the rebellion of the teen years is directly related to this smothering, limiting structure of controlled learning. But once your name is on a diploma, we apparently believe that you automatically receive an upload of knowledge (apparently bestowed on you by the wind or a band of friendly wood spirits) that will enable you to easily survive and thrive in the complex, hierarchical, and chaotic world of full-time work.

But that does not happen. The only difference between the last day of your college life and the first day of your professional career is that you become someone's employee. Not much happens beyond that. Therefore, it is only fair that you, the newbie to the world of work, get some insight into what can help you solidify your career and, hopefully, avoid the pitfalls so many encounter during their first year.

Notice I said "solidify your career." Will what I share make you a CEO tomorrow? Nope. Will considering my advice make you quickly realize lofty dreams of financial gains and wealth? Eh…no. Will your prowess and new found insight have you returning triumphantly to your alma mater as "Alumni of the Year" in just a few short months? Absolutely not. I offer insight into how you can start building the foundation of your career that will help you become successful down the road. This includes AVOIDING the mistakes (sometimes called 'derailers' as symbolic of a train that jumps off its tracks and comes to a grinding, screeching stop) that can cause your foundation to crumble. We will also discuss some things outside of work that have the potential to negatively affect your foundation, but that you may have never viewed as being potential problems.

The bulk of this book will not focus on specific skills but will look at behaviors. Skills are knowledge and abilities you have and use to get things done. Behaviors are instinctive reactions to things that happen to you or because of the environment around you. I am not concerned about skills with this book because skills can be taught rather easily and quickly. For example, if you do not know ANYTHING about cooking, and I ask you to fry an egg, chances are you will not do it very well. But if I show you the particular cooking skills related to frying an egg, you will likely be able to replicate those skills and fry an egg yourself in a short period of time. You may not do it well, but you can apply the skills you just observed to complete the task.

Behaviors are much more complex. I cannot tell you how to behave and expect you to pick it up in a matter of hours just by watching me. How you behave comes largely from the way you are wired, not from any lack of information on your part. One of this book's purposes is to illustrate that there are effective and ineffective behaviors you need to be aware of during your first year, so you can avoid being derailed by them. As an extreme example, let's suppose that when you disagree with someone, you react by yelling and screaming. Obviously this could become a problem in an environment where people need to work well together to get things done. I can explain to you that you need to be calm and not yell at people when you disagree with them. You may even agree with me and say that next time you disagree with someone you will be calm and not yell. But when subsequently faced with someone you disagree with, you react by yelling at them. Why did you react this way? Did you purposely lie to me with no intention of changing your behavior? No. Your behaviors are instinctive, so you simply reverted back to your comfortable, familiar behavior when you reacted to the situation. But after THIS yelling fit, you stop and realize what you have done and that you are not behaving in the manner in which you should be. You are now more aware of this particular behavior than you were before we began.

This self-awareness will help you to unlearn ineffective behaviors so that you can begin utilizing effective behaviors. The next time you face someone you disagree with, you may react angrily OR you may react calmly if you recognize the situation and manage your behavior in time. As you keep the effective behavior in mind, your behavior should begin to shift over time. In my opinion, the first year of your first job is the best time to become more self-aware of your behavior and compare it to what does or does not work within the work environment. If you discover you exhibit a 'derailing' behavior that you need to change, it will be much easier to make the change now than after you have been working (and exhibiting this behavior) for several years.

As you begin reading, think of this book as a study guide of topics for a test you are about to take, the test being the first year of your first job out of college. While not all the areas we will discuss will be on the final exam, you will not know which ones will or will not be included. In other words, you will not know which situations you may or may not encounter during your first year. So, the best strategy may be to study and become comfortable with every topic we discuss...just in case they are on the final exam.

Ready? Let's begin.

Section 2 – Building a Solid Foundation

LEAVING CAMPUS

2.1 Education – Round II

As we begin this journey, let's talk about a common misconception that I have seen among new graduates and why you need to be aware of it. Simply put, your education is not complete. Wait a second, you say. I just spent several years of my life, thousands upon thousands of dollars and countless hours of stress to get a degree just to find out I am not through learning? Well…yes.

You only received part of the equation during your years of school. Academics do an excellent job of teaching basic fundamentals and theories, but what they do not generally teach are the elements of risk and surprise. Those you learn on the job. School allowed us to assume away surprises to make sure we learned the fundamentals without becoming confused by random, unexpected variables.

You probably had several tests in school where the problem you were given said something like "Assume a rate of return of…," "Your patient is presenting an erratic heartbeat with limited verbal response…," "Your class is comprised of 50% structured learners and 50% experiential learners…," etc. Academia permits you to make certain assumptions about things that simplify what the end result would/could be.

For example, let's say there is a question as to whether failing to water a flower for fourteen days during the summer will cause it to die.

LEAVING CAMPUS

In the academic world, you can assume that the following will occur during the fourteen day period:

1. It will not rain;
2. The temperature will be ninety degrees or higher; and
3. The flower will not have any shade.

You will have to answer this for yourself, but you would probably agree that a flower in these conditions could whither and die. Now, let's look at the same question, only this time we also have to take into account what actually may occur with this flower in the real world. In the real world, we will have a flower and we know that we will not water the flower for fourteen days. However, the factors that we previously assumed as controlled now become uncontrolled. In other words, anything could happen. Let's look at our assumptions again in light of how reality affects our question about watering the flower:

Academic assumption: It will not rain.
Reality: It may or may not rain.

Academic assumption: The temperature will be ninety degrees or higher.
Reality: The temperature could go above ninety degrees or it may stay below ninety degrees.

Academic assumption: The flower will not have any shade.
Reality: The flower may be in direct sunlight or the skies could be cloudy during the period.

Again, you have to answer this for yourself, but I could argue that any of these factors could interact in such a way that the flower lives...or they could interact in such a way that the flower dies. You do not know. You now have to deal with an element of the unknown in your decision, which is "How will all these elements ultimately interact to affect the end result?" You will not be able to determine exactly what could happen before you make your decision. The best your decision can be is a calculated guess about how all of these elements may interact to produce the final outcome.

No one at your job is going to be able to give you a list of assumptions for the problems you will face with a guarantee that no other element will come into play before you have to make a decision...or after you have made a decision. Some schools (predominately business schools but certainly not limited to that) work from the concept of case studies where you are given historical situations with most of the elements that were known at the time. You are then asked to provide a solution. If you experienced case studies in college, hopefully you and your group worked hard, analyzed all the elements, and presented a position that was acceptable to the professor. Useful work, no doubt, but what I want you to be aware of is that these case studies rarely shock you with an unknown that could destabilize or destroy your entire effort.

The problem with this learning approach is that the majority of things in your life from this point forward will not come out quite the way you expect. Even many work days will end up being different than what you expected when you arrived at work that morning. So since your job will not function like a case study or a simulation where all the factors are controlled, and you do not have any experience with this "surprise" element, how do you adapt?

Don't forget, you did acquire some valuable basic knowledge in school. This knowledge is comprised of the "fundamentals" and "theories" your college professors taught and used in their project assignments and case studies. Depending on the situation you are faced with, you may be able to take the knowledge you gained in school and adapt it to your work issue. If so, you can move on to the next step of trying to solve the problem or address the issue and you will not be bothered by the element of surprise in this situation.

But if you cannot make heads or tails out of the situation using the knowledge you have, do not be destroyed. Instead, seek out some of the 'real world' knowledge from more experienced peers. They have been down this road and will be able to offer perspective to help bridge any gap between academic theory and real world application.

One way to identify your sources of 'real world knowledge' is to determine who does what in your area of responsibility and assemble a list of contacts that includes each individual's area of expertise. If you encounter an issue that demands immediate attention and you do not know what to do next, you can reference this list to determine who you should contact first for assistance. Knowing your "experts" saves a great deal of time and can help you solve the problem/make a decision more quickly.

Understanding where you can quickly access general information related to your line of work is also very helpful. The information source will vary based on your career field, but there are likely one or more resources you can identify. For example, you may use one of the many online reference databases for recent case law if you work in a legal or law-related area. If you are in the medical area, you may need to access a pharmacology guide from time-to-time to get specific information about drug interactions. If you are in accounting, easy access to accounting standards guides may be of use to you. Anything that can get you information quickly will save you time and increase your efficiency for your clients. Identifying your people and data resources in advance is a way to be prepared for the unexpected. You may still be caught off guard from time-to-time, but knowing what to do next or where to go for help when you need it lessens the impact of surprise.

Learning to trust your instincts to evaluate situations is another skill you must develop to deal with the unexpected. Education is a wonderful thing but, as mentioned, it engineers us to expect a fact-based absolute answer to whatever problem we face. Life does not give us problems with absolute answers and neither will your job. Your teachers and professors asked you questions and expected you to give them the answer they wanted; an absolute answer. Textbooks provided us with information that implied exactness for how a situation would resolve itself; again, an absolute answer. Expecting to find an absolute answer is something you will have to UN-learn as you begin your professional life, because rarely will you encounter complex situations where the answer is completely obvious.

I wish I could give you an exercise that would help you quickly develop your instincts, but I can't. Your instincts must be honed through real-life work experiences, most likely by screwing up a few times. Developing your instincts will be even more critical as your career progresses because you will have less time to make increasingly significant decisions that will impact you, your colleagues, and your employer. It is an odd irony that the more serious the decision, the less time you may have to make it, but that is a common characteristic of higher-level jobs. It is best, therefore, to begin honing your instincts early in your career so they will be ready when needed.

You will most likely misread more situations than you get right when you are first starting out, but don't be too hard on yourself when you do. Experience is the only way to develop your instincts and you have to DO something to have an experience. As long as you take lessons from any failures, you gain a great deal. If you try to rationalize your mistake and completely disregard your experience, however, you will lose out on a tremendous learning opportunity. Plus, you will likely make the same mistake again. Making a mistake once, it is a learning experience, but if you make the same mistake twice, your boss may think you have a performance problem.

As you gain more experience, you will start to look at situations, determine what needs to be done, and use your instincts to identify what issues take priority and which ones don't. I call this your "working eye." Developing your working eye is critical because you cannot address everything at one time so you need to prioritize what issues to address first. You cannot spend time worrying about every detail about every crisis or problem. You will not have the time, and frankly, you will not have the emotional energy.

As you have gathered by now, your new world of work will differ dramatically from your school life. How can you start building an effective foundation for your career that ensures both an effective transition from school and the development of positive work behaviors going forward? In the next section we will discuss some effective practices to help you through your first year. I am not saying these are ALL the things you need to know, but it is a start. Remember, we are building your foundation, not your whole house. Your house will take years to complete if you do it right.

2.2 Be Indispensable To Your Boss

The first stone you should add to your career foundation is to always be indispensable to your boss. Understand I am NOT talking about saying the things you think your boss wants to hear. That does not make you indispensable – it only makes your boss feel good. Instead, I am talking about the actions you can take.

One way to be indispensable to your boss is to deliver what is needed. The problem with that statement is that you may not know what is needed unless the boss sits down and expressly tells you! You could guess, but I don't recommend it. If your boss is not bringing up the topic, take the initiative and bring it up yourself. Explain that you want to make sure you are providing your boss what is needed. Have a list ready that outlines what YOU think the expectations and needs are and ask your boss if your list is accurate. Due to an overbooked schedule or other distractions, your boss may be better able to comment on a pre-existing list than to come up with one independently. Ask if your list captures everything that is needed or if you can add a few areas of responsibility. It will not be as hard a conversation as you think because you are telling your boss you want to make sure you are doing the right thing. That is a good message to send. Your boss will see that you have a genuine interest in delivering results and that you are willing to make the effort to make sure all bases are covered. You may not realize it, but you will also get a benefit from this conversation; that is, information about what is expected of you in your job.

Another way to be indispensable is to not criticize your boss to others. He or she needs to feel that if there are any problems or issues within the group, you will come to your boss first. People (especially other managers) tend to get a bit edgy when they see behavior like this because it begs the question, "If you ever worked for me or we had to work together on a project, are you going to tell the world all MY faults and failures?" As with any organization, the grapevine lives and your words could most likely flow back to your boss. Then what will you do?

Other examples of indispensability are delivering quality work on-time, being a positive member of the team, being customer focused and following through on requests and other behaviors that we will cover over the course of this book.

Why is it so important to be indispensable to your boss? Short-term, it's simple: you get to keep your job. Bosses tend to hold onto people they can count on and who deliver results. They tend to let go of people who either do not deliver results or cause them enormous problems and headaches. Indispensable employees make a boss' life easier. Longer term, however, indispensability can positively impact your future.

Elephants and the people who can affect your career have incredible memories. While a boss's memory may be a bit sketchy about the days you made his or her job easier, you can bet it will be remembered when the days were difficult because of you. Those memories could be taken to the grave. You never know how high your boss may move up the career ladder, so it is prudent to make sure any memory of you will be positive. One day your boss may be in a position of great influence. If it is recalled you have given them a favorable impression, they may think, "I remember *<insert your name here>*. S/he was really a good worker and I could always count on that person to do a great job. I need a _____ *<insert whatever high level position you aspire to here>* so maybe I will see whether that person would be interested in this opportunity." Your current boss could play a big role in your career at some future time, so be as indispensable as you can in the here and now.

2.3 What Am I Supposed to Be Doing?!?!?

One of the first questions you may have starting your first job is, "What am I supposed to be doing?" It is a reasonable question. Hopefully you will have a boss who will provide you with some significant one-on-one attention during your first few weeks to help you become comfortable with your role and what you are supposed to be doing. Many companies have structured performance management programs to help you understand what is expected of you. These programs gather very similar information to what you collected from your boss through last chapter's expectation discussion: guidance about what your boss needs you to do. Performance management programs go by a variety of names and, as long as they are properly utilized, they are highly effective in helping you know what you are supposed to do and deliver results.

Most performance plans begin at the start of the calendar year when the company business plan has been finalized and the executives have their goals. Typically, your boss will sit down with you and the two of you will identify goals that you are to accomplish throughout the year. The goals should be specific tasks or projects that are within your realm of responsibility, with a few that may stretch your abilities an inch or two. Good goals will be a clear, concise, outline of what is expected, and give a timeframe by which they should be completed. For example, an effective goal would be:

> *Establish and implement a procedure for tracking incoming prescriptions to show time of arrival, shipper, and*

originating pharmacy. Ensure communication of the procedure to all nursing staff so they are aware of what to expect and their role in the process. This procedure should be operating by the end of May of this year.

Over the course of the year, you and your boss should meet at least once (or even quarterly) to monitor your progress on your goals and determine whether any adjustments to your goals or the timeframe are needed. Business needs can change over the course of the year so you never know when funding for a project may disappear or something else takes priority, pushing one of your original goals off the plate. When this occurs, the goal needs to be either removed or noted as to why it no longer applies. During these goal discussions, you should also get an idea about your performance up to this point, to know whether or not you are doing the right things the right way.

At the end of the year, you should get a review that looks at your performance over the course of the entire year. This review should take into account your ability to deliver the goals you set out at the beginning of the year, and should include any other behaviors your boss observed, as well as any initiatives you assumed and accomplished that were not part of your initial goals. You may even get some type of performance 'rating.' I have seen ratings comprised of everything from letters (A, B or C) to numbers (1, 2 or 3) to classifications (Does Not Meet Expectations, Meets Expectations, Exceeds Expectations). Once the review is complete, you should get the opportunity to add your comments or feelings about the review to the final document. You and your boss will then sign-off on the final version, and you are done!

While this performance review will be for a specific performance year, it will have several purposes over the course of your career. In the short-term, it may serve as the basis for determining whatever raise and/or bonus you get (if you get a bonus this early in your career). Longer term, it could serve as data for a manager considering you for an open job in his/her organization. Often times hiring managers want to read performance reviews or see the performance ratings of potential employees before they consider interviewing them for an internal opening.

This is one area where moving around within a company differs from seeking a job outside the company. Internal hiring managers can get more information about you (both good and bad) than external companies can, and it is perfectly legal to do so. Keep this in mind whenever you add your personal comments to your annual review. You never know who may read them, so keep them reasonable and, where possible, unemotional.

Another part of the performance management process should relate to your personal development. I strongly believe that a large piece of your development and growth will come from on-the-job experience, hopefully, under the tutelage of a boss who practices good coaching skills. A good boss will want to make you more than you were yesterday and will take the time to reinforce successes and talk through challenges you face. Over time, he or she not only gives you work direction but tries to grow your abilities. These bosses view their job as 50% getting business results and 50% developing people. Under a supervisor like this, you will gain the benefit of their previous experience, and since they are a level above you, you should also gain insight into what it takes to move ahead at your organization.

Your boss may want to develop a plan that outlines the areas/topics that may need more development, how you will develop (or improve) them, and when the development should be complete. For example, a development plan could include a narrative similar to the following:

<u>*Area for Development*</u>

> *Develop familiarity around international operations and begin gathering knowledge of international business issues related to our company.*

<u>*How This Area Will Be Developed:*</u>

> 1. *Schedule meeting with Jack Preen, Managing Supervisor, International Operations, to gain an overview of ABC Company's international operations. Complete by the end of Q1.*
> 2. *Attend seminar focusing on general international business issues sponsored by National Business Seminars Inc. in Dallas. Complete by the end of Q2.*
> 3. *Participate on project teams focusing on deals with international business elements. <Boss> will seek out and identify opportunities that would best fit <your> current skill set. Complete by Q4.*

This is an example of how an area in which someone may need more development (knowledge of international operations) could be documented within a development plan. But development plans can also focus on where you are trying to go professionally and the actions you are going to take to get there over the next two, five, or ten year period. This timeline is much farther out than the one year or less timeframe addressed by the performance management process because you need time to develop yourself. For example, a position you aspire to could require you to get two or three years of additional training before you are qualified for it. The earlier you identify these training needs, the earlier you can find and take the training, and the earlier you will be qualified for the position.

You can easily put together a development plan for yourself if one is not included as part of your employer's performance management process. In fact, I would suggest you consider developing a basic career development plan after you have been in your job a year or two, as it can help you determine your next move and identify what knowledge or training you may need to get where you want to go from a professional perspective. Why?

Because employers like to see employees who have an idea of where they want to go and how they are going to get there. Having a plan also gives employees a degree of control over their career. I am always happy to counsel and coach employees about how to explore various career options and understand how one role may fit them better than another role. But I have to draw the line at employees who simply want me to develop a career path for them. If you do not know what you want, why do you think I do?

Why are we going into such detail on the topic of performance management? As much as I would love to tell you that your career and personal performance will be expertly and exactly managed by senior management from start to finish, I cannot. In some situations, you may be the only person who manages your performance and development. You could have a boss who receives no direction from his/her boss about what is expected of them, so they do not feel the need to provide you with any, either. You could have a boss who is very uncomfortable with one-on-one situations or is uncomfortable providing direct, candid feedback, so they avoid the process all together. Or you could have a boss who is so busy or has so many direct reports than he or she cannot do much else than say, "Great job! Keep up the good work," which though polite, is about as effective as eating soup with a fork.

Even if no one sits down with you and explains what you should be doing, you are still expected to do SOMETHING since you are taking up space in a job. The concept of "No one told me what I was supposed to do so I will just sit here" will not fly unless you genuinely just want an excuse to quit or be fired. So how do you figure out what you should be doing?

There are a few things you can do on your own to mirror the 'ideal' performance management process. The first one we've already discussed, which was to understand your boss' needs. Remember, we need to give the boss priority when it comes to your available time and energy because they hired you and can keep you employed, or make you unemployed. Once you understand their needs, what do you do next?

You will need to know what the people you support need from you. Over the course of this book, I refer to these folks as "clients" or "customers." These are people who need something from you to get their job done and they are a big reason that your job exists. Without their need for whatever it is you do, there would be no need for you to be around doing what you do. These can be internal employees, external customers, clients, other people's bosses, your co-workers and your support staff. Your customers' needs can be just as important as your boss's needs, so understanding and meeting their needs should be a high priority.

How would this type of conversation go with your customers? Actually, not much different than the conversation you had with your boss. You are telling your customers or clients that you recognize they depend on you for something (a report, counseling, data, or computer support, whatever) and that you want to make sure their needs are met. Ask them how they use what you provide and how you can best meet their needs. They may give you a significant amount of detail, or they may say something like, "You are doing just fine. Just keep doing what you are doing." Whatever the response, you have made it clear you want to meet their needs and are open to doing whatever it takes.

No matter what form it comes in, performance management is a key philosophy for you to consider placing in your career foundation. It will help you understand what you are supposed to be doing, how you should be doing it, and how well you did it once you are done. Hopefully your employer will utilize either a formal or informal process to guide, coach and direct you to be the most you can be. But if not, you will at least have the basic process we just discussed to help you set your goals and development plans to ensure your future success.

2.4 Building Bridges

I travel frequently in my job, and because travel is such a big hassle, I really notice the effort when an employee of a car rental agency, an airline or a hotel goes out of their way to make my trip easier. I'd like to think they do this because they think I am a great person and want my life to be stress-free. But the truth is they are trying to build a productive relationship with me, their customer, so I will come back and see them again… and bring my credit card. My return business is the benefit of their building a relationship with me.

As we talked about in the last chapter, you also have customers: the people you support. What benefit will there be for you to build productive relationships with your customers, and how will you build these relationships? My experience has shown me there are two benefits to building good relationships with the people you support:

They are happy because you deliver what they need. This is important because you will gain an objective resource who can tell your boss that you are doing a great job. These folks are serving as your performance documentation and an objective record for your boss indicating that you are contributing, and contributing well. Even if your employer has a structured performance management system, positive unsolicited feedback from customers tells your manager that you are making an effective effort to deliver.

You get good service in return. In every job I have held, I have tried to meet the needs of the folks I support. In return, these folks were very responsive to me whenever I needed anything. It is the old saying "You take care of me and I will take care of you" come to life. But some people still do not understand the relationship between how you treat people and how they treat you in return. I worked with one lady who was notoriously late delivering her data, never returned calls and emails on a timely basis, and sometimes failed to keep appointments made well in advance. She would then turn around and complain about how unresponsive people were to her and her requests. HELLO? You reap what you sow when it comes to dealing with people. She was one who sowed poor service to others, yet did not understand why she reaped the same in return. Do you understand the relationship?

In today's "me, me, me" world, it is refreshing to find someone who is more concerned about their customers' needs than their own. If you make an effort to build relationships with your customers, they will find this extremely valuable. The value of what you bring to a job will be measured by the people who use what you bring or the service you provide. Listening to what your "end users" are saying will build the type of relationship that will pay dividends back to you again and again.

In a previous chapter, we noted that two excellent sources about what is expected of you in your job are your boss and the people you support. There is nothing wrong, however, with having a similar conversation about expectations with your co-workers. With co-workers, the focus of the conversation will be more around personal interactions between you and them than meeting their needs. This conversation would include, "How can we best work together?"

Your peers may not be responsible for setting your goals and expectations, but they can tell you what behaviors are acceptable and unacceptable to them. Behaviors like honesty, dependability, follow through, etc., may not be goals, but your co-workers know which behaviors they value and how they expect a member of the team to act. Understand the world from their perspective and interact with them accordingly, and you may find your transition from "new person" to "teammate" is easier than you anticipated.

You may learn from these conversations that people are not necessarily going to think or be like you, although you may already know that. Knowing how people differ from you is valuable information, and I am not talking about differences you see. I believe that differences in people evolve from behaviors and needs, not from how we look or where we've come from. Your physical appearance can differ from the person standing beside you in a crowd, yet you may share very similar behaviors and needs with that person.

If you have ever taken a very long car trip with a friend, you probably learned quickly about any differences between the two of you. For example, your friend may have talked constantly while all you wanted to do was stare out the window and daydream. Their physical appearance did not matter – all you were focused on was their constant talking. Differences between one person's needs and another person's behaviors can create conflicting situations when they are opposite. You can imagine that if you were thirsty and I gave you a glass of salt water, I would not be meeting your need. My behavior (giving you a glass of salt water) would not meet your need (the need for water you can drink). You probably would not be very happy with me.

Realizing that people may exhibit behaviors and have needs that differ from yours is a first step towards building effective working relationships. You should think of yourself and others as puzzle pieces: sometimes the edges will fit together and sometimes they will not. One piece is not better or worse than another, they are just different. If you have ever tried to put a puzzle piece into a section that it was not designed for, you know it is a futile effort to try and force a fit. Instead of forcing a fit, learn what the differences between the two of you may be. See if you can understand why they may need something other than what you first offered, or why they behave differently than how you expected (or needed) them to behave. Understanding the facts behind the behaviors should help you find an effective way to work together and also show the other person that you are willing to make the relationship work, even if differences exist.

Sometimes good relationships require you to put a piece of yourself out there before the other person feels comfortable enough to meet you halfway. But once you see how to make a relationship work in this manner, you will have gained a valuable asset that you can use throughout your career. Your professional success requires the contribution of other people, as we will discuss in the next chapter.

2.5 Big We, Little We, Not About Me

In college, YOU were primarily responsible for what you did and how you were graded. YOU studied for YOUR test that culminated in YOUR grade for the class. You may have had a few group projects where a portion of your grade was affected by how your peers rated your contribution to the team, but for the bulk of your college career, you were flying solo when it came to your studies. As long as you participated in class, did well on tests and got your projects in on-time, you realistically could get a passing grade. It was all about YOU.

In your job, however, you will need other people to get things done. Granted, you will be solely accountable for a few things from time-to-time, but overall, there is not much you will be able to start or finish without the help of someone else along the way. The simplified model of work is that you:

1. Get work from someone;
2. Do the work, either by yourself or with the help of others;
3. Send the end result to someone for their use.

If you want to complicate your job, do a poor job in managing your relationships with the people at any one of these points along the way. If your relationship with the person bringing you the work is poor, you may not get your work on-time or receive everything you should. If your relationship is poor with the person receiving your work, you may not be able to hand off your completed work to them when it is done. Even doing the work can be a problem if you have poor relationships with those who can help you get the work done. But if you want to make your job easier, let's talk about a few things that can help ease your transition from the campus to an office, a hospital, a school, a lab or wherever you may roam.

First, think "we." Say "we." Act like "we." We, we, we all the way to work and we, we, we all the way home. It is not all about just you now. It is "we." "We" is inclusive. When you speak in terms of "we," it shows you are thinking beyond just your needs and glory. It also helps other people to see, think, and feel that you include them in your work-related thoughts, actions and plans. There are two good ways to use "we":

Big WE: This is applicable when you speak about a larger entity – the entire company, the entire department, the entire shift. Using "we" in this context demonstrates that we are all in this together and we are looking out for the good of the team by our actions.

Little WE: This is more applicable when you are speaking to someone one-on-one in a business setting. In a situation where there will be two of you involved, "we" indicates that we are in this together. "I have your back," "I am looking out for you," "I will meet your deadline." What you are saying is that success will be the end result of two sets of efforts.

You may think I am going a little overboard about "we," but I have found "we" to be a powerful expression of working effectively with others. I embraced the concept of

LEAVING CAMPUS

"we" a long time ago and have not regretted it. Since I have learned over the years the reality of needing others, "we" has helped me initiate healthy professional relationships and keep them productive and enjoyable for many years.

2.6 *I Do Not Know The Answer To That Question, BUT...*

When I started my career, a wise manager gave me this piece of advice: "If you do not know the answer, say you do not know the answer...but make sure you go find out the answer." You probably will not know how to answer many questions posed to you during your first year, but that is to be expected. What is important is how you handle that situation. No matter who is asking or what the question is, someone came to you for information and it is your responsibility to meet that need. To this day, I continue to be dumbfounded by people who, when you ask them a question, just tell you that they do not know. That is it. No follow up. No offer to find it out. They just..."don't know." I strongly encourage you to be honest and say "I don't know, but I will find an answer."

If you do not know the answer to a question, do not be creative and make one up. Folks who have been around awhile will know when you are lying/making it up. Dead giveaways are:

- You may stammer;
- You may not answer immediately;
- You may look around the room, searching for an answer; or
- You may launch into the ever popular verbal signal known as "Uhhhhhhh..."

LEAVING CAMPUS

I tried to "be creative" once. I was interviewing with a well-known company and was having my second interview. The first interview went well but the second one had the VP of Human Resources present and she was apparently having a bad day/week/life.

She was quiet for most of the interview and then she began asking the most bizarre, irrelevant questions. For her last question, she asked how many employees of each race I had at my location. Heck, I did not carry those numbers around in my head…there was not enough room. But being the creative type, I pulled a few numbers out of my head and threw them out on the table. Seemed like a reasonable answer and I was actually quite proud of myself. But suddenly, everything just died. Done. Over. She grunted "Thanks," got up and left.

When I answered her last question, I was certain she wanted to see how well I knew my organization. But now I realize she wanted to see if I would be forthcoming enough to say "I do not know" to a question that most people could not easily answer without research. So, my guidance is to just be honest. It is o.k. to not know the answer to something when you are just starting out as long as you acknowledge it, and follow up with the right information. A side benefit to searching out the question is that next time, you will know the answer and will appear to be quite competent and informed…as long as they do not ask you anything else you don't know!

2.7 Do What You Said You Would Do

A corollary to 'if you do not know, say you do not know but find out the answer' is: **FOLLOW UP WITH WHOEVER HAD THE QUESTION.** You will soon have enough confidence to say "I do not know." But if you do not find the answer and do not follow up with the person, what has the person gained by coming to you for help? Make sure you close the loop and meet their need for information. Not only will they get their answer, you will show that you have not forgotten their request and that you have a "customer focused" orientation (this means you look out for the needs of others with your actions).

The importance of following up and closing the loop is one of the first lessons I learned when I entered the working world. A wonderful shift supervisor wanted to pass along as much of his forty plus years of knowledge as he could before he retired, and he taught me this lesson. He knew that his hourly employees loved to talk about how "management does not care" and the "office people do not give a rat's behind about what the employees on the shop floor needed." He did not want me to become one of the "staff people" whom no one on the shop floor respected. He routinely reminded me about what my responsibilities were to anyone who had questions and needs; I needed to follow up. He was right.

As a result of his guidance, I began keeping a list of employees who either had requests or questions, and why they had called. I did not take their names off that list until I knew their request had been completed or their question answered. If I did not know the status of a request, I simply called the employee and asked whether or not their need had been met. Over time, I noticed an increase in the number of questions and requests that came my way from our employees. I figured out that people will bring you their needs if they honestly believe you will try to help them. Otherwise, they will not bother. People love people who have great customer support skills and follow through on what they say they will do...no matter how small the request.

You can probably think of situations when you needed help from someone but they either did not offer it or they offered but failed to follow up with what they said they would do. How did you feel? Once people discover that you get results, you may see requests for your assistance increase. That is a good thing, as being busy equates to increased job security and indispensability. In the downsizing-oriented world of today, that means something.

2.8 *What You Dish Out*

With any hierarchical system, there are levels of authority and responsibility. The higher someone is in the hierarchy, the more power, authority and responsibility they possess. In some organizations, there may be a tendency by certain individuals to "look down" upon those who are at lower levels of responsibility in the organization. When you begin to look at someone as their job and not as the person they are, you are falling into this trap. Such a mentality shows itself when leaders in higher level roles ignore or poorly treat those who are in lower support roles (by lower support roles I mean positions like administrative assistants, secretaries, janitors, security guards, etc.) Do not follow the lead of such "leaders" when it comes to how you treat people in roles lower than yours. Why?

1. It is wrong for a litany of reasons related to our roles as human beings;
2. You will miss out on a valuable source of insight and perspective because these folks will not want to help someone succeed who treats them poorly, and
3. These folks can be your best allies, and in some cases (i.e., executive assistants) they hold a lot more power than some misguided middle managers give them credit for holding.

For example, let's look at executive assistants. They are not the executives, but many DO keep the extra keys to the suite/restroom/parking spots. They are the ones who may handle the calendars of your boss, your boss's boss, and your boss's boss four times removed. Many executive assistants and secretaries have the ears and <u>trust</u> of key folks around the organization and can affect certain perceptions of you in both good and bad ways, depending on their interactions with you.

See the point of avoiding elitist (you think you are better than someone else) behavior? Foster the relationships with everyone you have contact with, no matter what their role or level to you. You treat them well and you will get the same in return. Mistreat them, and you do so at your own peril.

I will close this chapter with a story. One Fall we spent several days interviewing MBAs for our company's very lucrative training program. A large number of our senior managers (including the president) and human resources staff were gathered in a large boardroom reviewing each and every candidate to determine who would receive a job offer. We were down to two virtually identical candidates for our last available position. Both candidates were from good schools, both had similar qualifications and both had performed very well in the interview process. Discussions went back and forth but it was impossible to gain a consensus because they were so much alike. Finally, the president said, "Ask Cindy to come in here, please."

Cindy was the receptionist who greeted each and every visitor who came into the company's front lobby and was also responsible for arranging transportation back to the airport for the MBA candidates. Our president asked her, "Do you recall either of these two candidates?" and described each of them. "Did you have any interaction with them?" he asked. She indicated that she recalled them and was alone with each while they waited in the lobby for their ride to the airport. He then said, "Which one of these was nicer to you?"

According to Cindy, one student had been very polite and courteous, both upon his arrival to our building and as he waited for his ride. He asked how she liked working for our company and a few other small talk questions. The other candidate, however, barely looked her in the eye, except when asking her where the restroom was located and *telling* her to throw his coffee cup away. Otherwise, he simply ignored her.

The first MBA received the job offer.

2.9 *Watch Your Tongue*

When I was a less experienced HR Manager, I used to dread discussing difficult issues with employees. By difficult issue, I mean anything from negative news about themselves (i.e., their failure to get to work on-time is creating a problem) to a request that would obviously inconvenience them in some way, shape, or form. I just knew they would be either defensive or angry and it made my stomach turn to think about the conversation. After all, none of us enjoy messages which frustrate us or cause us to have an altered view of our competence. While we cannot change the truth if the truth is indeed negative, I have learned there is a way to help reduce the potential discomfort that comes from having to confront someone about a difficult situation. It is simply to understand that how you deliver a message affects how it is received by the person on the other end.

Think back in your own experiences. Do you remember when you screwed up as a teenager and your parents would begin their barrage of "I cannot believe you blah, blah, blah" and "When I was your age, I would never blah, blah, blah?" If you recall, it was not the message itself that got under your skin (because hey, we really never listened, anyway); it was the way they delivered the message because it made you feel like a child again…and you did not like that, did you?

Regardless of their age, people can still become upset if you talk to them like they are children…or dogs…or idiots. No one likes to feel belittled by someone else. Though your message may be perfectly valid and clear, people ARE more likely to hear how you are delivering your message than what you are actually saying. When I have two employees in a tiff, I frequently hear one of the employees say "You should have heard how he/she was talking to me! It was like I was an idiot. I am NOT an idiot. I am sorry *<the mistake>* occurred but I did not appreciate being spoken to in that way." I rarely find out the details of the situation (i.e., what happened) until much later in the conversation, after the person has calmed down.

If you have a difficult message to deliver to another person, rehearse how you might deliver it and then think about how it may be interpreted. For example, let's say the message is "You are not sending the reports on-time" or "You are making it difficult for me to get my work done," or maybe it is "You have not been very responsive to my requests." These are very direct statements that point out that the person to whom you are speaking is at fault. I am a big fan of being direct with whatever I have to say because there is less chance of the message being misunderstood. But by using "you" and making the issue personal, you have gone to a different place. You may not intend it that way, but when you use "you," people can take that personally. By phrasing the issue this way, you attack them personally and honestly, the issue really is not about who they are as a person.

Instead of focusing on who is at fault, focus on the issue that is creating the problem. For example, let's say you need a piece of information from someone but you are not receiving it when you need it. The issue in this example is that you are not receiving the data you need in a timely manner. Explain to the person that there is a piece of information that you need to be able to do your job, but you are not receiving it when you need it. You would like to see if there is any way that you can get the information when you need it. You understand that they are responsible for providing the information you need, so you have come to them to see if they have any ideas about how this could be accomplished. With this approach, you go from blaming them to focusing on the situation to make it work better. Your message now says "I do not care whose fault it is. Let's make this work."

Don't let your message get lost in translation because your style is putting someone on the defensive. Remember, people first hear and see how you are saying something before they hear WHAT you are trying to communicate. For example, how are you coming across vocally? Is the tone of your voice agitated or condescending? Is your voice fast and forceful? Or are you calm (but firm), in a normal volume? The style and manner in which you communicate with someone is likely what you will get in return. For example, if you are aggressive and loud in your explanation of the issue, the person you are speaking with will likely react in the same way. When this happens, the chance of reaching a solution to the issue diminishes.

Remember you do not always know what is going on in the life of the person on the other end of the conversation. Maybe they have just received some bad news or they have personal issues that you have no idea about. None of this has anything to do with you. But if the manner in which you present an issue to another employee could cause them to become defensive, it could be the catalyst that pushes your co-worker over the edge, resulting in a defensive or hostile reaction.

If you are wondering whether you could have a style or manner of speaking that could be misinterpreted by others, talk to people who've known you for awhile. Tell them you need to know whether there is any way you could improve the way you interact with others because it is critically important in your job. Ask them whether there are things you do, or ways you react, that may make them uncomfortable when it comes to discussing difficult topics with you. Be sure you give them permission to be as blunt and honest as they can because you want the feedback. Otherwise, they may be reluctant to be as honest and as open as you need them to be. Since we are building a career foundation that is to last for many years, we need as much honest, constructive feedback as we can get to make sure we are on the right track.

2.10 *Your New History Lesson*

In the last chapter, you were giving feedback to another individual. Now let's change places and have you be the person receiving feedback, only this time the feedback is not negative and is incredibly valuable. It is what I call Historical Coaching, and it is the transfer of knowledge from another point in time to the present. You are the recipient of it tax-free. I will explain.

I have always been fascinated by the lottery. The idea of spending a dollar and choosing a combination of numbers that could provide you with a financial benefit for life is amazing. When I was younger, I wanted to find a magic book that contained every winning lottery number for the next twenty years. With that information, I would win every lottery I chose to play, no matter when or where it was played. I could take care of myself, my family and anyone else I chose to without having to worry about the financial obligations of life. With that magic book, I would be financially secure in the present.

In Historical Coaching (HC), you receive something just as valuable as a magic book of lottery numbers, if you choose to look at it that way. Historical Coaching occurs when someone who is more experienced than you provides you with insight, lessons, and observations from their past history that they think may be valuable to you in the present. Most of the time you will find HC is triggered by a specific event: you may have been involved in a situation this individual observed or maybe had heard you were involved in a particular project and decided to share personal thoughts and experiences as a result. But HC can also occur without warning. The really good Historical Coaches will start off on a totally different subject and somehow wind up in a story or tale that cleverly comes back to whatever point is desired to be made. It is akin to watching a sail boat glide across the water only to circle back to its original position and stop. You find yourself transfixed and feel as if you have taken a journey without ever leaving your position…and you gain some useful information as a result.

Early in my career, I made a presentation to a group of senior managers where I outlined my plan for an upcoming job fair. I felt strongly that some of the senior managers needed to be present at this event to help attract candidates and indicated this to the managers in attendance. At the end of my presentation, the group indicated that they agreed with what I wanted to do for the job fair but did not see the need to have senior managers present. I was instructed to find an alternative course of action to what I had proposed.

I was somewhat disappointed and to a degree, angry, at their rebuff of my recommendation. This was going to be a big event for us and I wanted it to succeed. I could take care of all the logistics but the main indicator of success would be the volume and quality of resumes we would receive from the job fair. In my mind, potential candidates would be impressed at the sight of senior managers present and willing to speak with them about careers at our company. Why would these managers NOT come? It seemed like a great idea.

Later that day, I had a visit from one of the managers in the room that morning named Mike. He had come to tell me that he thought I had put together a good plan for the job fair and that the point I made about senior managers being present was a good one. I thanked him but said that I obviously did not make that good of an argument since none of them would be attending the job fair. Mike smiled and said he understood how I felt as he had been in that situation many times before. Then he shared a story from his past.

Years earlier, Mike had happened upon a great idea for a tool that would help his maintenance employees handle some difficult valves more easily. On his own time, he drew up plans, tested various configurations and even paid to have a prototype made when his design was finalized. With great pride, Mike took his design and prototype to his manager with the expectation that the company would see the value and want to invest in its production and development. His manager, however, turned the idea down. The manager explained that while it seemed like a great idea, the company was not in the business of tool research and manufacturing. It just was not something they knew anything about. Dejected, Mike left his manager's office, threw the prototype into his garage and let it sit for many months.

Later that year, one of the tool suppliers that regularly visited the plant heard about Mike's prototype and asked to see it. Mike gave it to them to study and a few weeks later, he sold it to this company for a good price and a percentage of future sales. At the end of the day, his situation worked out, it just was not as he had planned.

I thought about Mike's story for a few days and realized there was a better option than what I had proposed. I initially wanted senior managers present at the job fair to give our company clout and appeal. But would these managers be able to tell potential candidates what the jobs required? Maybe at a high level, but candidates like to know details and specifics about what jobs entail. I realized that a senior manager sitting two levels up probably would not have this information. Who then could provide this information to candidates at the job fair? The people doing the jobs!

I recruited employees who had experience in each of the jobs we needed to fill and had them available for questions at the job fair. It worked beautifully. Candidates who were interested in working for us found out exactly what our jobs required and had all their questions answered by my "resident experts." I learned that there is more than one way to accomplish a goal; you just have to be willing to explore all options and not give up until you find the one that fits.

Historical Coaching is a great way to bridge the gap between school learning and real world application. More experienced employees like to share their past experiences, and you can benefit from this knowledge. In my experience, the knowledge gained from more experienced co-workers taught me more than many classes I had in college. From their stories, I was able to take bits and pieces of their experiences and file them away as options to consider for future situations. I have benefited from their suggestions several times over the course of my career. Their experiences also enabled me to develop my "working eye," meaning the ability to look at a situation and prioritize what was critical, what was not, and what else I needed to know before I could solve the problem.

Too often we may view people who have worked for several years as being "out of touch" or "not current on the latest things." In some ways, that may be true, and unless someone is actively keeping their skills and abilities current, they can be using systems, methods or processes that are a bit dated. But while they may be a little behind in their knowledge of current theories and methodologies, they are well ahead in knowing how to make things work in the real world. Take whatever Historical Coaching is provided to you, or seek it out if you identify a more experienced employee you feel has a high degree of competence in your same field, and see what you can gain from their knowledge. The latter concept is called finding an "Unknowing Mentor," and we will discuss this concept in the next chapter.

2.11 The Unknowing Mentor

You may ask, "What is an Unknowing Mentor and what am I looking for in an Unknowing Mentor?" Let's start by explaining the concept of mentoring. Some companies utilize formal mentoring programs that pair less experienced employees (mentees) with more experienced employees (mentors) for the purpose of sharing knowledge. Mentors provide mentees with coaching, suggestions, and tips about things to watch out for in their job, ways to grow a career, etc. from the perspective of someone who has been there/done that. Mentors are typically not the mentee's supervisor, because supervisors need to maintain an equal interest in/ /responsibility for everyone on their team. If a supervisor was spending more time coaching/developing one particular individual over another, it could be construed as favoritism by the rest of the team. This could hurt the team's ability to work together.

The intent of a mentoring relationship is to provide the mentee with someone to help move them along their career continuum and to be a sounding board for whatever questions, frustrations, or successes the mentee may have. The concept of an Unknowing Mentor functions a bit differently from a typical mentoring relationship because the "Unknowing Mentor" does not know they are mentoring you! You could schedule a meeting with them and let them know that you are glad they are your mentor and you are looking forward to getting to know them better. But I don't advise that. Your Unknowing Mentor will not have a formal role in your development, but they will make a significant contribution. Being able to observe them and how they behave in the environment will give you a great deal of information to consider and use as you see fit.

I started using this method very early in my career and I was able to pick and choose various behaviors and skills from my Unknowing Mentors that helped me create my own personal style. One individual I used to work with always had managers and supervisors in his office talking over various things. I wondered, "How can I build the same rapport with people?" What I observed was that he was a good listener. When presented with a problem from someone, he did not solve it for them (although he easily could have) but instead he asked for background about the problem. How did you get here? What led to this? What else has been done? The person with the problem would talk, and as they talked, my Unknowing Mentor asked more questions. The person would start to see there were some options out there. They just needed someone to help them realize it, and my Unknowing Mentor did this by listening and asking questions.

Another Unknowing Mentor taught me how to deal with executives in an effective yet respectful way (which can be difficult from time-to-time). This same mentor also had a practice of owning a person's problem until it was resolved. When it was necessary to pass along a request to someone else, she always told the requestor to come back to her if they did not get follow-up within a reasonable time. She would continue to carry the issue forward until the person was satisfied. Both these individuals were viewed as highly competent within our organization, motivated by the right things, and fit the culture of the company. I have been able to take their lessons, adapt them to fit my own style, and grow a bit faster professionally than if I had had to learn those lessons on my own.

Now that we've defined the Unknowing Mentor, where do we find one? Hopefully you will be able to find one or two potential candidates within your workgroup using the process I am about to describe. My process identifies folks who have habits and behaviors worth modeling that can lead to success in a career. I need to point out that my definition of success is not acquiring power, prestige and money but being a balanced, contributing and growing employee.

Over the years, I have started to evaluate people against three different factors. I like these factors because they are blind to any demographic indicator (race, gender, etc.) and can be measured by simple observation. I am sharing this because once explained, I feel this is a tool you can use to evaluate potential candidates for the role of your "Unknowing Mentor." What you want to find in your work group/team/department, etc. is a person who demonstrates the positive aspects of each of the three areas I am about to explain.

The factors I use to evaluate people are:

1. How well they do what they do **(Competence)**
2. Why they do what they do **(Motivation)**
3. How well they fit within their employer's culture **(Fit with the Culture)**

I define each of these in the following ways:

Competence: This is the easiest of the three to define because it describes someone who is technically good at what they do. There will usually be someone who by reputation is the "best" or one of the "top performers." It may be the customer service rep who consistently receives high numbers for customer satisfaction, the sales rep who consistently meets or exceeds his or her targets, or the staff person who handles problems quickly and efficiently. In other words, the person knows his or her stuff and has a reputation for excellence. You can determine who meets this requirement through conversations with your manager, your peers or other folks within the group.

Your boss' and co-workers' opinions are equally important to your observations for this factor. Some individuals may LOOK like they know what they are doing, but they do not follow up with results or the results they provide are inaccurate. A friend of mine used the term "tennis whites," to describe an employee who looked good but could not play. If you have ever noticed someone who is dressed in the latest gear on the ski slope, beach or tennis court but who looks totally lost when they are trying to ski, surf or play tennis, you understand what I am talking about. Your manager and co-workers will have a very strong opinion on someone like this. Any employee who talks a good game but does not deliver results impacts everyone in a negative way and usually has a reputation as such.

Motivation: Short of talking to the person to find out why they do what they do, you have to start depending on your judgment for this factor. With motivation, we are looking for someone with a work motivation based on the understanding of responsibility and the desire to deliver what they are supposed to. The best co-workers I have had were ones who understood that they had certain responsibilities and they carried through on those responsibilities because people depended on them, or because they held themselves to such a high standard of performance. These folks put a little bit of themselves into their job – not because their job defined who they were, but because they knew that whatever they did reflected back on them. They wanted to show their capabilities. If they could not deliver as promised, they made sure that you recognized such and that your needs were taken care of by whomever could do the job.

The folks who do not meet this factor are the ones who just come to work because they need the paycheck and will probably hang around until something else happens (layoff, termination, death, the lottery, etc.). They are really not interested in whether or not you get what you need or whether you get answers to other questions. If they are late with something you need, they are late. If you do not like what you received from them or what they did for you? Tough. They just work here.

You will not gain anything from observing these folks.

Fit with the Culture: This is one you will definitely have to gather from observation and it may take awhile to figure out who fits the culture. But people who fit the culture you work in carry some of the best information Unknowing Mentors can offer about how to survive in your current environment. Company cultures are defined by people, and since people are all, by nature, very different, some people thrive in certain cultures and some don't. The people you see growing within a company are the ones who have responded well to the company's culture, whatever that may be. Cultures tend to replicate themselves because if one type of person does well in a culture, and that culture is made of people like them, they tend to bring other people like them into the culture, and so on, and so on. This can be both good AND bad.

People with successful behaviors can bring in people with successful behaviors and conversely, people with unsuccessful behaviors can bring in people with unsuccessful behaviors. You have probably heard about "cultural change" and how it is SOOOOO difficult...almost impossible. Cultural change is difficult because there are usually a small number of people trying to convince a large number of people to change the way they think and act. It is not easy because the majority liked the way things were, and now this small group of voices is asking them to change. Without a compelling reason to change, folks tend to like to stay just as they are.

As stated, all companies have their own cultures. If someone has been with the company for awhile and has moved up and/or is viewed as successful, chances are they demonstrate behaviors that are consistent with the company overall. For example, if the company has a culture that desires action and the individual is one who seems be always on the go and is in the midst of many things, it would likely be a good cultural fit. Or, if the culture values hierarchy, respect for levels and titles, and the individual seems to have fostered respectful relationships with those at higher levels and knows how to manage those relationships, they fit the culture well.

Individuals who do not fit with the culture will stand out to you. Someone who may not fit appears to always be at odds with people, either through their words or through their actions, may not speak favorably about the company and/or their role in it, or behave in a way that does not seem consistent with the general environment. An example of the latter could be someone with a loud, boisterous communication style working in a company that is relatively low key and polite in its interactions.

Based on this brief explanation, I hope you understand how an Unknowing Mentor could be beneficial and how you can find one. You can have many Unknowing Mentors over the course of your career – there is no limit and you may find them to be an easy way to broaden your own capabilities with minimal effort. It is definitely a subjective call about who you choose to make your Unknowing Mentor, but the good thing is you have no downside to giving it a try. No one will ever know. If you follow the above guidelines, you may be pleasantly surprised by what you learn.

2.12 *Why Do I Care About Company Culture?*

Before we move on, I want to spend a little time explaining the concept of "company culture" and what it looks like in the real world. It can be a difficult concept to explain because a company's culture can be described five different ways by five different people - each person's description based on their own perceptions. There will be common themes among the five descriptions — factors that all five people will agree are in the "company's culture." But there will also be some differences based on an individual's position in the organization or experiences that affected their perception of the culture. Finding one definition that everyone can agree on is difficult. So why are we spending any time on this? Because a company's culture can have such an impact on you and your success/failure in a job that I think it is important that you have at least a basic definition of "company culture."

For starters, a company's culture is much greater than just its physical workplace. "Company culture" is the aggregate of all the environmental characteristics and behaviors that people who are members of a company agree to conform to in order to remain members of the company. If you took a sociology class, you may remember that cultures are born when a group of people, or a "company" of people, come together to work for a common goal. In prehistoric times, a common group goal may have been survival through communal farming or hunting. In today's world, we have groups ranging from hospitals to schools to large multi-national organizations where people come together to heal, to teach others, or to produce products around the world. Each of these groups, or companies, will have their own distinct culture. For now, let's imagine that "company culture" is a keyhole with a specific size, shape and set of mechanisms that are necessary to open the lock inside. How are these characteristics of the keyhole, or the culture of the company, determined?

Many things can affect and shape the culture of a company, but to walk through all the possible factors and blends that could form a company's culture would require a book unto itself. Characteristics such as the age of the company, the industry in which it operates, the complexity of its product line, size, and financial strength of the company are just a few factors that can combine in various ways to affect a company's culture. Let's look at a couple of environmental factors and see how they could affect the formation of a company's culture. We will choose two factors that are relatively easy to relate to: size and financial security.

Thanks to the American capitalist system, there are businesses of all shapes and sizes. The smallest could be run by one person on a part-time basis from the basement of his home. The largest could employ hundreds of thousands of people, be in several countries, and be worth billions! How can size affect a company's culture? Let's look at the differences between a large city and a small town to understand the impact size can have, and then we will apply what we learn to company culture.

Maybe you have walked along a downtown street in a large city and observed all the activity going on around you. Did you see the people filling the sidewalks, hurrying to their next destination? Did you hear the orchestra of sounds, from bus horns to train cars shuttling passengers from K Street to West Avenue, and the whistles of cops directing traffic? Did you smell the scent of hot dogs from the street vendor's carriage or the waft of car exhaust from the lines of cabs waiting at the light? All these elements come together to help define the culture of a city, at least from a sensory perspective. If someone talks about 'the city,' this may be what you envision. It is your reality about how a city looks, smells and acts.

Maybe you have walked along the sidewalk in a small town – what did you see? You probably did not see the same crowd of people moving en masse along the sidewalk as you did in a large city. In fact, you may not have seen a soul on the main street of this small town for several minutes or longer. What sounds did you hear in this little berg? You likely did not hear traffic horns and cops blowing their whistles, but could you hear the birds singing or the bell in the church tower ringing noon? What did you smell? You may have picked up the scent of a fried pork chop sandwich from the corner diner or the smell of fresh cut grass from the house one street over from where you were. You may have caught a whiff of the cow pasture not too far outside of town. If someone talks about 'the small town,' this scene may be what you envision. It is your reality about how a small town looks, smells and acts.

Assuming you are someone who lives their life at a relaxed, unhurried pace, let's place you into these two environments and see how you fit. How well would you be received in a large city slowly walking down the packed sidewalk, leisurely stopping to smell whatever living flower or plant you could be lucky enough to find growing out of the concrete? My guess is someone would say, "Hey! You may not be in a hurry, pal, but I am. Get out of my way!" as they pushed you aside and sped down the sidewalk. Your leisurely style may not fit with the hurried, energetic pace of your sidewalk companions in the large city. But in the small town, your laid back, check-out-the-world-as-it-goes-by style may fit right in. You may even be too fast for the locals and they have to tell you to slow down!

Now let's apply this same scenario to you and a company's culture. If you are someone who is relatively laid back and unhurried about getting things done, and you work for a company where everything is driven by schedules and tight deadlines such as a newspaper or construction company, you may feel out of place. The way you are (laid back) is the complete opposite of what the culture requires (scheduled, structured), and you may feel the difference. Or, if you are someone who must be constantly busy and always on the go, but you work for a medical research company where the slow, methodical style of research dictates the pace of action within the company, you may be a bit uncomfortable...even unhappy. You will not be able to get what you need (a constant high level of activity) from the environment the business offers (steady and methodical).

Another factor affecting a company's culture is the financial strength of the company. Have you ever run to the grocery store, shopped the crowded aisles as screaming children darted in and out of the shopping carts, loaded up your little basket, waited in the line with people who thought thirty items were close enough to ten for the express lane, put all your purchases up on the checkout belt only to find you had NO MONEY! That's right! You had no money and no checks! Do you recall how you felt? The 'sickness in the pit of your stomach' feeling when you cannot think of anything but how black and empty your wallet or purse is at that particular moment?

But then there are positive financial moments, too, like when your bills are all paid for the month and you find you have more money in your checking account than you thought you would at that point. If everything goes as planned, you should come out a little bit ahead for the month. It is a nice feeling, a secure feeling, one that does not make your stomach hurt.

Employees can experience these same roller coaster feelings depending on the company's financial situation. If a company is teetering on the brink of bankruptcy or every other year it announces a new wave of job cuts, the culture can be ripe with distress, fear and anxiety...a negative environment. If a company manages its finances well, the culture may have elements of confidence, security and an orientation towards the company's future growth...a positive environment. The financial strength of a company will not be the only factor that determines its culture but it can have a significant impact (either positively or negatively) on the company's culture.

Size and financial strength are just two examples of the environmental factors that contribute to a company's culture. Now let's look at two businesses with two different focuses to further define what "company culture" looks like, how it can vary among companies based on their line of business, and how the characteristics of the business can affect employees.

Our first example will be a manufacturing-focused company. Manufacturing companies create success for themselves by producing a quality product. If you were a business student and took production/operations management classes, you may remember that good production processes are precise, repeatable, monitored and consistent. This enables the company to produce products that meet customer expectations over and over again. In order to know whether their production process is operating as it should, manufacturing companies focus on data and precision.

If it is a chemical company, it may pull samples from its manufacturing process and test them to make sure they are within an acceptable range of quality. If a company produces engines, it may pull a motor from the production line, break it down completely and measure the size of each valve against what the quality standard says it should be. If a company produces gasoline, it will have many different meters throughout its plant measuring the temperature and pressure of the crude oil at various stages of processing to ensure these levels remain within safe limits to avoid the potential of an explosion.

This data dependency and need for precision carries over into the "company culture" of a manufacturing company. You will not find many situations where people make decisions based on "gut feel." Instead, you may need to provide supporting data about why your recommendation is the optimal solution, no matter if you are requesting an increase in your capital budget or trying to get a new coffee pot for the employee cafeteria.

Companies like this can also be more apt to develop "analysis paralysis," the condition where you can ask for and analyze such a large volume of data that you end up moving very slowly or not doing anything at all. Why? Because the volume of data is so large that it points you in several different directions without a clear cut path. You can infer so many things from the data that you do not know what to do next. Precise supporting data is expected for major decisions, but you also see this need for data showing up in personnel reviews, salary changes, travel expenses, and even payroll cycles.

One company I know of paid employees every two weeks. Most companies divide annual salaries by 26 to reach the bi-weekly gross pay amount. That seems reasonable because hey, there are 26 pay periods in a year when you pay every two weeks! This company, however, divided annual gross pay by 26.09. Why? An engineer within the company determined that an extra pay period occurs every ten years as a result of the leap years. Therefore, in order to be 'exact' with what employees were paid (over a lifetime, I guess), they elected to use a denominator of 26.09. Did the data support this? Technically, yes. Did it drive some people crazy? Yes. But it was just a part of the culture of being precise.

Our other company example will be a marketing or sales-focused company. Marketing and sales focused companies usually promote a brand or service to the public in order to gain business and make money. They usually sell products that are not significantly different from the products their competitors sell (i.e., tissue paper), so as a result, they have to make consumers understand (and believe) that their product is the one they should choose as it is better than anything else out there. Marketing is the best way to get this message across.

The "company culture" of a marketing company is generally dynamic and fast-paced due to the need to quickly adapt to a changing marketplace. Marketing companies tend to have less rigidity and structure because too much structure can increase the amount of time it takes to respond to a market opportunity. If a company moves too slowly, it may miss an opportunity to enhance its market share or market position. Likewise, processes and discussions that consume too much time will not be easily tolerated, and may even be ignored, as they are perceived as slowing the business down.

You will also find a very competitive culture within marketing companies. A company's competitive position can change daily, so the people who lead and hold higher level positions must have a need to stay on top and win. As a result, employees with the most "wins" in their area of expertise are the ones who get noticed for future promotion and advancement opportunities. Folks are more likely to be highly competitive in this type of company, and the company benefits from this characteristic. There is not much time to sit back and enjoy the fruits of a 'win' in a marketing company, as your competitor will be at your heels (or worse, passing you by) if you sit and gloat.

These two examples about company types and their cultures are only intended to illustrate how the culture of a company can be affected by the type of business it is in. In the manufacturing example, we described a culture that is data-driven, steady and methodical...characteristic of its manufacturing operation. In the marketing example, we described a culture that was fast paced, driven and competitive...much like the business of marketing and sales. Neither culture is better or worse than the other, but each is different, partly because of their respective businesses.

Let's recap where we are. We have defined "company culture" as the environment that employees agree to conform to in order to remain members of the company. We looked at the effect of size and financial stability as two examples of how various environmental factors can contribute to the formation of a "company's culture." Finally, we looked at two different businesses to show how cultures can be affected by their line of business. In a very basic sense, we have illustrated how keyholes, or company cultures, evolve.

Now we need to look at the key, or the human element, to see how well it may fit, or not fit, within the company's culture, or the keyhole. The key is basically the person we are. The things we like and do not like, how we behave, what motivates and what de-motivates us. All these factors, and more, form our individual "key." When a person fits a company's culture, everything works effortlessly. Their performance is solid, they slowly take on more and more responsibility, they build healthy, productive relationships, and they have a feeling of satisfaction from their employment. Everything clicks, just like when the correct key goes into the matching keyhole – the key fits, it turns easily, the tumblers are moved, and the lock releases its hold on whatever it was securing.

But when a person does not fit the company's culture, nothing seems to work without a lot of effort. Though they try hard, they do not seem to meet the needs and expectations of their boss or customers, they seem to struggle with the basics of their job, they are not building the relationships they need to get their job done, and they do not feel like they fit in. Just like when you put the wrong key in the keyhole, no amount of effort will make that key turn and lock release. The key and the keyhole do not fit together. For our purposes, "company culture" comes down to this simple question: how well does someone fit (or not fit) the culture of their company?

I have seen the "bad cultural fit" play out time after time. It is one of the reasons people move out of a company after being in a job for just a short while. If a person does not complement the culture (or vice versa), it is not likely that the professional relationship will work out very well. For example, I was involved in the hiring of a tremendously talented functional manager for one of our larger departments. Everything fit – skills, employment experience as it applied to the job we were trying to fill, industry contacts, everything. Everything except, as we found out later, the company culture.

Our company operated on a team philosophy. While each person had differing levels of responsibilities (and, of course, differing titles), everyone interacted on a personable, team-oriented basis. It was an environment of mutual respect where everyone wanted the company to succeed. The issue with this particular manager was that she felt she needed to operate from a position of personal power to be effective.

She needed to feel that everyone knew her level and title in the organization, and she expected the people who interacted with her to respect that level of authority. In other words, people should become submissive to her in most circumstances. In our organization, this just did not happen. People did respect the responsibilities that higher level employees had and were rarely disrespectful. But you were free to disagree, for example, with an executive who chaired a committee on which you served because it was for the good of the business. At the end of the day, though, the executive had to make certain decisions, and everyone respected that.

This individual had apparently never had someone subordinate to her, question a topic for which she was responsible. When one finally did, the situation about sent her into orbit. This was not the only situation where the problem surfaced. The behavior exhibited itself even when someone called her by her first name (which was customary in our company). Needless to say, her time in our company was brief and luckily for her, she was marketable enough to find a new role on her own in a very short time. I certainly hope her new employer was much more formal in their respect of title and level than we were!

With company culture, you simply need to understand that the person you are (made up of a variety of wonderful, diverse factors combined in a multitude of ways) will sometimes fit the culture of a company perfectly, and sometimes will not. It is just the way things are. Your key will fit some cultures better than others. It may take a few years (or even a few jobs) before you are comfortable articulating the environment that works best for you. But at least being introduced to "company culture" at this stage of your career raises your awareness about a complex area that will exist in your work life for many years to come.

2.13 *The Unwritten Rule of the Day Is*

E very company or organization has a set of unwritten rules that the members of the organization follow...consciously or not. I have tried to give examples for most of the topics I have covered in this book, but I am limited as to how much guidance I can give when it comes to unwritten rules, without knowing your specific organization. Unwritten rules seem to be in all companies, though, and likely involve things that make you think, "Why is that a big deal?" They are not called unwritten rules because the company is making a conscious effort to conceal them. Instead, they are called unwritten rules because they are beliefs or norms that exist within the company, but since they are not published anywhere, they will not be obvious to you at first glance.

Unwritten rules can exist for any topic. There can be unwritten rules related to how you address people at the executive level. Greeting folks on a first name basis may be permissible or you may be expected to refer to everyone by "Mr." or "Mrs." or "Ms.", depending on their status. There may be unwritten rules related to when you should be at work every day. Your employee handbook may say that core work hours are from 9:00 AM to 5:00 PM. The unwritten rule, however, may say that since the CEO arrives at 7:30 AM each morning, all staff are expected to arrive at 7:30 AM. Following are a few examples of unwritten rules I have experienced over the years so you can get an idea of their almost eccentric nature.

LEAVING CAMPUS

A friend of mine worked for a large public utility for many years. The company was headquartered in a tall, beautiful, glass-encased structure that towered above the local skyline. The top floor housed all of the senior executives (referred to as "The Top of the House"), and there were two ways to reach this floor. A beautiful, curving staircase reached up from the floor directly below the executive level and brought you into the very center of the executive area. Or, you could take a dark, institutional stairway that doubled as the fire escape and brought you out next to the bathrooms on the executive level. Which would you choose?

My first reaction would be to take the central staircase. Both options take you to the same place so why not go in style and enjoy the view? WRONG. The unwritten rule was that you never took the central staircase up to the executive floor unless you were directly invited to a meeting with an executive or taking something to an executive. Period. If you just needed to drop off a package or pick up a memo, you must take the other staircase. My friend had no clue about that until she did it wrong the first time! In her case, the only adverse effect that came from her not knowing about this 'unwritten rule' was a counseling session from her manager not to do this again. But sometimes the result can be a bit more serious.

At another company, the unwritten rule had to do with relocating and its effect on your career. As a large multinational company with many locations, positions would open up around the country which the company had to fill. They had a practice of filling the better opportunities with internal candidates, then backfilling that open job with either internal candidates or external candidates. In my opinion, that is a good practice since you give your internal folks the first shot at the best opportunities. If you were asked by a senior manager to take one of the open jobs, you had two options: take it, or turn it down. Either option was o.k. If it was the right position for you, in a good location, and your family situation would permit you to uproot and move your life from Point A to Point B, that was fine. If the position was NOT one that you particularly aspired to, or your situation did not permit you to relocate at that particular time, that was fine, too. The company was flexible.

So what is the unwritten rule? The unwritten rule came into play if this situation came up again. If you were tapped by the "Almighty" for an open position a second time, you really just had one choice: take the job. If you did not take the position, you ran the risk of moving out of the "favored" pool into the "we think they no longer have serious aspirations here" pool of candidates, a much more crowded and grumpy pool of people. People usually found out about this rule when they told their immediate supervisor for the second time that they were not interested in taking the position...sometimes when it was too late to reconsider.

The last example is about a rule which rears its head during the hiring process and concerns an external candidate's response to a job offer to join a particular company. As you know, the United States is a free nation where its citizens have many rights. One of these rights is the ability to sell their services to the highest bidder, usually in the form of a salary or hourly rate. Whenever a company makes an offer of employment to an individual, part of that offer includes what the person will be paid. Once the offer is presented to a candidate, it is not unreasonable for the candidate to ask for a little more salary than what was initially offered. It is simply negotiating: you do not know what is possible until you ask. Worst case the company says 'no', best case the candidate gets a little more than he or she would have otherwise.

When this particular company makes an offer to a candidate, however, negotiating is not allowed. If the candidate comes back and asks for more money, the offer is pulled off the table and the company is done with the candidate. Why? I have no clue. I do not even know how to explain this one, but apparently it is a standard practice and it happened to an acquaintance of mine. He interviewed at this company and after receiving a reasonable (but not stellar) offer, asked for a slightly higher salary. The company then pulled the offer and they were done. I later received confirmation from some of my peers in the recruiting community that this was a standard practice at this company. Why a company would invest the time and energy in a search to find the right candidate for a job, decide they want them, make an offer, then pull away the offer because the candidate simply attempted to negotiate is beyond me. But that is their practice and in my mind, their unwritten rule.

These are just a few of the examples of 'unwritten rules' that companies have, and I am sure there are more. I would suspect wherever you end up working probably has a few unwritten rules, and if nothing else but for a good laugh, it would be a good idea to try to find out what they may be after you have been on the job a few months. Start with your boss. Tell him or her that since you are becoming more involved with the company and your position, you wanted to know whether there are any 'rules' or 'practices' that are not obvious, but that you need to know about. You can feel free to give the above examples as your own if that will help. Your boss may have no clue what in the world you are talking about (because they themselves may not know), but at least you asked.

If your boss does not have any insight about your company's 'unwritten rules,' bring it up with your co-workers or your Unknowing Mentor or even the person who recruited you into the company (if it was someone other than your boss). At least one of these folks should have a story to relay about the unwritten rules within your workplace and how best to deal with them.

In closing, I wanted to provide you with a silly blurb that illustrates how the unknowing new employees can be affected by existing unwritten rules that they had no idea about, but get sucked into just the same:

> *Start with a cage containing five apes. In the cage, hang a banana on a string and put stairs under it. Before long, an ape will go to the stairs and start to climb towards the banana. As soon as he touches the stairs, spray all of the apes with cold water. After a while, another ape makes an attempt with the same result — all the apes are sprayed with cold water. Continue until another ape tries to climb the stairs, and the other apes will try to prevent it.*

> *Turn off the cold water.*

> *Now, remove one ape from the cage and replace it with a new one. The new ape sees the banana and wants to climb*

the stairs. To his horror, all of the other apes attack him. After another attempt and attack, he knows that if he tries to climb the stairs, he will be assaulted.

Next, remove another of the original five apes and replace it with a new one. The newcomer goes to the stairs and is attacked. The previous newcomer takes part in the punishment with enthusiasm.

Again, replace the third original ape with a new one. The new one makes it to the stairs and is attacked as well. Two of the four apes that assaulted him have no idea why they were not permitted to climb the stairs, or why they are participating in the assault of the newest ape.

After replacing the fourth and fifth original apes, all the apes that were sprayed with cold water have been replaced. Nevertheless, no ape ever again approaches the stairs. Why not?

"Because that is the way it has always been around here."

Writer unknown

2.14 Ready – Aim – Deliver!

One of the hardest things to wait for when you are fresh out of school is a chance to show what you can do. While we would all love the opportunity to bound straight off campus and into the CEO's office with a backpack full of fresh, exciting ideas that blow everyone away, that rarely happens. A less senior manager, however, or maybe even a slightly senior peer, may give you a chance to demonstrate your skills. When this happens, you need to recognize that you are getting your opportunity. Even though they may not be the most senior person in your organization, they are just as important as one higher in the organization. Why?

With your service to that individual, your public reputation will begin. No matter what their level in the organization, you need to treat all your clients and customers with equal importance. How well (or poorly) you support that person will most likely be shared with others at some future time. This sharing of information can occur in many ways. It may be they have input into raises, promotions, etc., or that they, despite their lack of title, are respected by more senior staff and are frequently solicited for their input on various topics. If you do your best possible job with this person and show your capabilities, they become your unknowing "publicist" or "marketer" when they let other people know they went to you for help and got results. You develop a reputation as someone who gets things done in the organization, which will start to drive more business opportunities your way. With increased business, you will now have more opportunities to demonstrate what you can do and show off even more of your talents. As long as you recognize these opportunities and do the best that you possibly can when they are presented, you will make the most of these chances.

What does "your best" look like? Doing "your best" has five core components:

> **Be optimistic and have a "can do" attitude:** There are enough people in your client's life that will state a "no" or that something "cannot be done" and offer no alternatives. You need to be one who sees the possibilities instead of the impossibilities. Do your best to understand what your client's need is and use this information to form your solution to meet the need and assist with the resolution of the problem. If you cannot do exactly what the client has asked you to do, indicate you are unable, at the time, to solve the problem but propose an alternate solution or offer to come back with options after you have had a chance to do some research. Take your client to a better place than before coming to you for help.

> **Never neglect details:** When someone asks you to do something, repeat their request back to them to make sure you understood it correctly. If you need to, write it down. This way, you are that assured you understand what they need and will not forget a critical piece of information that could cause you to waste time and appear careless to your client when you show them your results. It is a disappointing feeling to work long and hard on a product only to

hear your client say, "Well, that's not quite what I had in mind."

Deliver on what you say you will do: When you commit to specific actions with a customer, you need to deliver what you have promised because that person is assuming you will. Do not assume that your customer will not care if you do not deliver the results when promised. If you cannot meet your customer's expectations or time-frame, discuss this with your customer. Be sure to understand the difficulties that will now be experienced as a result of your failure to deliver. If there is something you can do to alleviate the situation, by all means, do it. You are still responsible for making sure the need is met. It may not be you that ultimately takes care of the problem or delivers the solution to the problem, but you should be the catalyst that brings your customer together with his/her solution.

Believe you can do it: Remember the story of the little steam engine puffing up the track, trying to make it up the hill? At the end of the story, he makes it simply due to his own sheer will. You hold a very powerful tool that you can either use to contribute to your success, or your failure. It is your spirit. When you encounter difficult situations, you need to hear yourself say two phrases: "I can do it. I will do it." Repeat it over and over if you have to, but say it. You can just as easily think, "I'm toast. It's over. I will never get this done." which we sometimes say to ourselves without realizing it. Do not give this or other negative phrases a chance to enter your mind. Show yourself that you believe in yourself and it will give you more of a boost than you might expect.

Take the time to double check your work product: We are a fast-paced society and the characteristic of fast service has become a standard expectation. When we were younger, it would take weeks to get a toy from a mail order catalog after sending off the form and our parent's check. Now you can go online, click a few virtual buttons, enter a credit card number, and have your toy tomorrow (or faster if it can be downloaded). When it comes to the work product you are producing for someone else or the service you are providing them, being speedy is great, but this is not a race. Take a little time to go back through what you have done and make sure it is complete before you hand it off to the customer. Careless errors can create a perception that hurts your product's credibility. Obvious errors such as misspelled words or a calculation that is just a little off due to those pesky decimal points may make your client think, "Well if that is wrong, what else about this is wrong?" If the product is shoddy, its value is diminished. A few minutes of double checking can save your credibility.

Unfortunately, I have been involved in a lot of employment terminations over the years, especially when my companies have had to eliminate jobs. Through this experience, I have observed where the above characteristics come into play. Even though these are not skill-related characteristics, they ARE highly valued by managers. They are actually more valuable than basic skills because you cannot put someone in a seminar or class and have that person come out "doing his or her best." Folks either get this concept, or they don't. When forced to choose which of their employees would be terminated as part of a company cost cutting effort, I have seen managers do whatever they can to keep the employees who demonstrate the above behaviors (i.e., they do their best as described above). These factors are that important to employers.

2.15 *Conciseness Is a Virtue*

In my work, I see two styles when it comes to communication: long and short. Some folks walk right up to you, tell you exactly what they need or what the problem is, and they are done. They are pleasant about it (most of the time), but aside from expressing what they need, there is not much else that goes along with that conversation. I call this the short style of communication.

Then there are other people who start out on one topic and finally wind up on a totally different topic, the latter being the reason they came to see you in the first place. I have spent many a time wondering "Where in the world is this conversation going?" before the person finally arrived at their point or request. I call this the long style of communication.

When you were in school, you may have had teachers or professors who graded you on how broad and deep your explanations were. The more words and explanations you used, the better your grade! Being from the South, I grew up where you cannot provide an explanation or tell a story without providing a colorful, yet appropriate, analogy that explains things like how much Junior ate at the church picnic ("He was as hungry as a suckling pig coming off a hunger strike") or why you will not get what you want ("People in Hell want ice water, too, so you can just keep on wishing"). But as much of a fan as I am of long, colorful language, I cannot in good faith suggest that you adopt a long communication style this early in your career.

LEAVING CAMPUS

Time is a precious commodity with many people, especially those in higher level positions. So much is crammed into a brief day (even for those folks who work ten to twelve hours straight) that they can barely address one topic before another one pops up requiring their immediate and total attention...and usually a quick decision. They only want a short list of bullets about what you need from them or a simple question they can answer so they can move on to other things. Your busy co-workers may not have the patience for long, drawn out explanations about why something did not happen or why you are showing up needing their assistance. They value clarity and conciseness, so just give them a synopsis if you need to provide them information or to solicit their help.

KISS is an acronym that can help you remember the preferred style to use with busy people: **Keep It Short and Simple.** If someone wants to chat a little longer or more in-depth, or has a few more detailed questions about your request/statement, then by all means, let the details fly. But in general, remember to strive for brevity and conciseness in your communications and presentations — you can always elaborate if need be. Since I value conciseness, that is all I will say about that.

2.16 *You Do Not Work in a Democracy*

Those of us who live in America truly value our freedoms. We argue, fight, protest, and in some cases even die, for what we feel is important. We can vote for leaders, make choices about our future, and basically choose to do or not to do just about everything we want (as long as it legal, moral and non-fattening, of course). That is the beauty of what our country is all about. Choices and the opportunity to effect change. Too many times, though, I find employees who get their Constitutionally-guaranteed rights mixed up with their more limited rights of being an employee. This leads to problems.

When we begin working for a company, we agree to perform a certain type of work for a certain rate of pay. We also agree (either express or implied) that we will follow the rules and procedures the company has established. Most people understand this, but some employees still think that if there is a portion of their job they do not like, then they have the right to either:

1. Not do it, or
2. Make a big stink to change it.

Let's discuss the first topic: refusing to do something you have been asked (or instructed) to do. In the military, soldiers and support staff follow direct, very specific orders intended to help the entire platoon/division/military achieve its objective. This unified movement is critical. If all were allowed to do whatever they wanted to do, or not do, there would be total chaos and the military's objective would not be met. Employers follow a similar philosophy. Companies move forward when everyone in the company is heading in the same direction doing their individual role as expected. Employers rarely dictate direct orders, but they do delegate work and assign responsibilities to employees. Delegated work and assigned responsibilities tell employees what they are expected, and required, to do.

The military has laws that dictate severe punishments for soldiers who disobey direct orders because following orders is critical to the military's success. Companies have similar rules or practices. If you are delegated a project or responsibility and expressly refuse to do it, you have committed insubordination. Insubordination is usually outlined in an organization's policies as being a terminable offense...meaning you can be immediately fired for it. In situations where you have a concern about what you have been asked to do, it is best to first follow through on whatever you were assigned (assuming the assignment is legal). You can then discuss any concerns you had about the assignment with your supervisor or manager AFTER you have completed the task. Do all organizations immediately fire all employees who are insubordinate? Probably not, but my guidance to you is not to test your employer to determine their position on the matter.

Now let's cover the second topic: making a "big stink" to change something you do not like in your workplace. The "big stink" I am talking about is not one of those big stinks created so the world will be better for all of us. Those stinks, such as those raised by Gandhi, Martin Luther King and the people who dumped tea in Boston Harbor, were intended to lessen the pain, tears and unfair taxes suffered by large numbers of people. Instead, the "big stink" I mean is one where the sole purpose is for one person to get what they want, all others be damned. This is called the "Me Stink" and the employees who raise the "Me Stink" are not usually your most valued employees.

These are the employees who do not like the idea of having to call and tell their supervisor if they will not be coming to work. It 'inconveniences' them. So, they just don't show up. They may not think being on-time for work every day is important or they may not see the need to offer their help to other employees if they are not particularly busy at a certain time. Why? These things are not convenient for them and they do not believe in being inconvenienced.

Most employees understand there are duties you simply have to complete to continue being employed or to have good relationships with co-workers. They may not like some of the duties they have to do, but they do them. The "Me Stinkers," however, will resist and complain about whatever they do not like and in many cases put their employment in jeopardy.

I once had a situation where two employees were not getting along. Not an uncommon problem, but it was disrupting the work group so I had an obligation to look into it. I spoke with the first employee, and after a long conversation I determined that he was becoming very frustrated with his co-worker because she was more interested in criticizing what he was doing than completing her work. It had reached the point where she was providing him with feedback about what he was doing wrong and how he could do it better. He had been in his job for several years and knew what he was doing and simply resented this intrusion by someone who was not his boss. Fair enough, I thought.

I spoke to the other employee and found out that indeed, she had been observing the other employee and felt that he just was not taking care of things like she thought he ought to. She felt that she was acting in his best interest by letting him know. I told her that I understood her intent but since her actions were disrupting the other employee's ability to get his job done, she would need to stop it. It would be up to the employee's manager to address any performance issues and as far as I was aware, there were none.

This just sent her into a tizzy. She was insulted that I would view her actions in a negative way and she felt she had every right, and even an obligation, to provide feedback to whomever she pleased. I explained to her that the company had a policy on non-harassment and while this situation was not sexual or racial in nature, it could be considered harassment because the co-worker was unable to do his job as a result of her behavior. The feedback she was providing was not welcome and she needed to stop. I then received quite a lecture about her skills, her abilities and her intent to continue doing whatever she felt she needed to make the work group better, after which she stormed out of my office. She simply believed she had the right to behave this way and was not going to be inconvenienced by someone telling her "no."

This little situation is an excellent example of a "me stink," where an employee did not understand the concept of "choosing battles wisely." Some issues in your job will be worth fighting for and some will not. In this example, what exactly does my employee get if she "wins?" Considering the fact that her actions are making someone else miserable, will that be viewed by others as a noble goal? It likely will not. She has already created a large amount of strife and consumed a great deal of many people's time for a self-centered goal that is of no positive benefit to anyone except her own ego. This is not a battle I would choose to fight and put my employment in jeopardy over...a true "me stink."

However, I believe the other employee did have a reason to raise a "big stink": to put a stop to harassing behavior that was impacting his ability to do his job. All employees have the right to work in an environment free of unwanted conduct in the workplace. Anyone who becomes subject to such behavior has the right and obligation to report it to the supervisor or the Human Resources Department and pursue it through the proper channels until it is corrected. While that is not a topic for this book, it is a prime example of a battle WORTH fighting. Over time, you will learn the distinctions, but for now, just remember that when you are in the midst of a contentious situation, ask yourself – Am I raising a "big stink" or a "me stink?" Is the end result worth it? Or will I lose more than I will gain from this battle?

In the case of our self-anointed performance coach, she created such chaos within her team she developed a poor reputation as a team member. She also developed a performance problem. She was so concerned about her co-worker's performance, and became so worked up about being told to stop coaching him, that she failed to get two key projects delivered on-time. Consequently, none of our project teams wanted her involved in their projects, so she ended up with nothing to do. When you do not have anything to do in an organization, your job becomes at risk. Each person needs to be contributing at a 100% level, but if you have no work to do, you cannot contribute. Since no one was willing to work with her and we were preparing to eliminate jobs for cost cutting reasons, she ended up being severed from the company. Sad but true.

If you find yourself embroiled in one of these fruitless "me stinks," but do not realize it until you are well into it, do not think you have to see it through to the end. Instead, consider the concept of "strategic retreat." In military action, armies sometimes find themselves in the heat of a battle where the best they can do is avoid complete annihilation. Victory is lost, but instead of fighting to the death and losing both the day and their lives, armies will pull back from the fight and retreat. This is called a "strategic retreat" because you are not running from your enemy out of fear, but instead you are retreating so you can fight another day.

It is never too late to back away from a bad situation and say "I am done – there is nothing I can gain from this." Stop and drop it. Your pride may try to tell you that you have failed because you did not see an issue through to the end, but do not listen. This is one situation where perseverance will not work in your favor.

2.17 *Change For The Sake of Change...or Not*

Now that you are working, change is going to be a constant part of your life. One year you will have a new boss, the next year new co-workers, and the next year your office may end up in a new building. Without change, everything will remain the same. You would not want your pay to stay the same from year to year, would you? In order to make situations better than they were, you need change. But change does not always mean things will definitely be better. There should be a logical reason behind any change.

For example, imagine you just completed a blueberry pie and now you want to make an apple pie. You check your remaining ingredients and find you have a pie crust, sugar, lemon zest and blueberries. You want to make an apple pie but the only fruit you have is a bowl of blueberries. What do you do?

You can either:

1. Give up on the idea of making an apple pie and go back to your old blueberry pie making ways, or
2. You can replace the bowl of blueberries with a bowl of apples and actually make an apple pie!

If you want or need to make an apple pie, you must change out your fruit in order to accomplish what you want to do. This is a prime example of a necessary change.

You will soon see that employers like to change things wherever possible. If there is an opportunity to save or make a dollar by doing things differently, employers will make the necessary changes. When things change in a work environment, everyone seems to notice because it creates a hope that the change will result in a better situation than that which existed before.

Recommending or actually making a change can be a great way for an employee to demonstrate the capability to make things better for their employer. But sometimes I fear new employees, and especially those "new to the working world" employees, feel as if they have to change something to demonstrate their knowledge and their abilities.

When I began my first full-time job, I bought into this need to change something and decided that all our policies at our plant needed to be updated. I went through all the policies, updated each one of them, and sent brand new copies to all of our supervisors. I genuinely believed that this would demonstrate some level of knowledge on my part and would not cause a lot of trouble. Boy, was I wrong.

The next day, I received several calls from my supervisors asking "What policy changes did you make? It looks to be about the same but we are afraid we are missing something." Actually, the policies themselves had not really changed – the intent and the language were much the same as they had been. What I had done was replace all the references to 'he' in the policy manual with 'she/he.' Yes. That is it. That is all I did. Would I spend the time and effort doing all that again? Absolutely not. I would not have the time and to be honest, the effort was not worth the result. This was an unnecessary change because the changes I made did not make the policies better or easier to apply.

My advice from that experience is do not feel as if you need to start recommending or making changes the minute you walk into the door of your new job. There are no bonus points for changing things within days of your hire date. When we are new to an environment or a company, we do not know how things are done and what the inter-relationships are between various people, departments, etc. It will take time to acquire this information and understand all the intricacies. Even high level folks brought in to make drastic changes to an organization give themselves time to understand how things currently work before they start making moves. They know they will not be able to make a case for the change they desire until they understand the current situation, how the change would impact others, and can explain to others why a change would be beneficial.

If you have the opportunity to suggest or make a change in how things work in your environment, make sure you understand the impact of the change before you make it. If you fail to do so, your change could make things worse instead of better. Take our apple pie example for instance. I do not know if you caught it or not (the bakers among you may have) but there was one additional change we should have made. You do not typically put lemon zest in an apple pie; you usually put cinnamon. Therefore, we should have changed out our lemon zest for cinnamon to make a true apple pie. If nothing else, we should have removed the lemon zest. Leaving it in the recipe could negatively affect the taste of your pie. If you noticed that little omission, good for you!

In a similar manner, trying to force changes in an unfamiliar environment could cause you to miss a key element that will cause your change effort to fail miserably. You are too early in your career to make avoidable mistakes, so until you have a good idea of how things currently work in your work environment, just roll with the flow for a little while. You may find that the way things are currently set up is about as optimal as they can reasonably be...if you just give yourself a chance to figure them out. But if you do find an opportunity to create a better future through a necessary change, you will be able to explain how the change can make things better because you took the time to understand the present.

2.18 *You Truly Annoy Me*

When you pick up a piece of recruiting literature from an organization, you always see a group of smiling, laughing people on the cover who just cannot seem to get enough of having their picture taken. They seem to genuinely like each other, too. If the recruiting information is to be believed, everyone you meet in that particular organization should give you a big toothy grin and wish you a good day. Wouldn't that be great, if everywhere you went, people greeted you with one of those big toothy grins and gave each of their co-workers one of those million dollar smiles as well? Wouldn't it also be great if everyone really liked each other?

Of course it would. But the truth is that there are some people in this world who just cannot get along with each other. In fact, you can probably think of one or two people you do not get along with very well, either. It could be for any reason: you/they could be rude, mean, too nice, slow, fast, arrogant, brash, polite, pretty, etc. for you/them to stomach and thus there will always be an overarching "thing" that would keep you and this person from forming any type of interpersonal bond. You likely may not try very hard to make the relationship better, either. After all, it is hard enough to get along with the people you LIKE on a daily basis; why spend the effort on someone you do not like?

In our school and personal life, we had many options to deal with these people. We could try and smooth out our relationship with them, but that did not always work. We could ignore them completely, or we could find every opportunity to argue with them about something of little or no consequence simply to aggravate them. Whatever option we chose, our lives were not significantly impacted if there was someone we did not get along with. It was our choice as to whether we had to see them at all, so we could usually focus our time on other, more enjoyable relationships in our life and disassociate ourselves from the others.

Unfortunately, you will not have as many options when you encounter a similar situation in your job. Whenever you put a large number of people in one place, you are going to have some relationships that do not work very well. It eventually happens to everyone. There will be a person you have to deal with on a regular basis with which you do not have the best relationship.

But remember, you agreed to follow the policies and procedures of the employer when you accepted your new job. One of the philosophies employers have (whether or not it is in writing) is that they pay their employees to get along. That is it. No negotiation there. You do not have to like the people you work with, but you are expected to get along with them and not cause problems within the work environment; otherwise the ramifications can be quite negative...up to and including losing your job. So what do you do?

You find a solution to poor relationships by following some key principles:

Know when you need to address an issue and when you don't. If there is someone you have to interact with on a regular basis, it is a relationship you cannot let degrade. You will have to address the dysfunctional situation; otherwise it could impact your ability to do your job. But if it is someone with whom you rarely interact or your contact with them is limited, then it is probably best to just ignore the whole situation. Yes, it may create a bit of annoyance and frustration in your life from time-to-time when you do encounter them, but so do flies and spiders, and you have survived up to this point in your life.

Understand this probably is not personal. It is just a work situation that is not working, for whatever reason. At this point in your career, no one at work knows the person you are deep down inside. They only know your work persona and behaviors; those are not what you are all about. It cannot be personal if they do not know you. Do not assume that it is, because most of the time you will be wrong and make a bad situation worse.

Make an effort to improve the situation. Approach the person, explain what the situation is from your perspective and ask if there is anything that you can do to make it work better. You may also explain what it is you need to get your job done and offer up a solution if one is needed. Be careful to avoid any criticism of the person (remember, do not make it personal); focus on the work issue at hand, and show you are willing to work with the person to make things better. This approach will have positive results most of the time. When it does not, though, you are about out of options. The only thing left to

LEAVING CAMPUS

do is to get help from your supervisor. Otherwise, you may find it difficult to get your job done because the other person simply refuses to cooperate.

It is never enjoyable to have a difficult working relationship with another employee, but the key thing to remember is that you cannot let the situation manage you. You must manage it because the situation will not get better by doing nothing. You may never reach the point that you and this other individual become friends, but if you can find a way to get what you need from them on a consistent basis, you will have gained valuable insight into managing difficult relationships.

Section 3 - Personal Realities

LEAVING CAMPUS

3.1 *A is for Accountability*

In this and subsequent chapters, I want to talk about situations where your personal behavior can creep into your work life in ways you may not expect. Things like: your behavior outside of work, your dating life, and the management of your finances. First, though, we need to talk about an overarching theme that affects basically everything about your first year on your own. It is called accountability.

The definition of accountability is that you are "responsible to someone for some action." A simple definition, but it is incredibly complex in its application. Your willingness to understand and accept accountability in your life will be critically important to your ability to function as a self-sufficient, independent adult going forward.

For most of your life, you were cared for by someone else (e.g., parents, grandparents, guardian, etc.) in some way, shape, or form. Over the past few years, you may have been living away from home, going to class, managing your spending money, etc., but there was probably some link back to someone else for direct support. If something came up that required money or assistance, you could just pick up the phone and they would take care of it. When classes were over for the semester or the quarter, you likely went back home, slept in your old bed, ate their food, and watched their TV. No matter where you were or what the situation, you had someone who could help you meet your needs.

Now that you are out on your own, you need to start adjusting to the reality that everything is up to you. Your world going forward is going to be defined by your decisions and actions, and the consequences that come from those decisions and actions. You can think of yourself up until this point in your life as someone bungee jumping with a safety net below. You get the thrill of jumping off into the unknown, but if the rope breaks or is too long, the safety net (e.g., "someone else") will cushion your fall and allow you to walk away unscathed. You make the decision to jump and enjoy the ride, knowing that if something goes wrong, you have a way out...a way to escape any negative consequences of your decision. Not any more. The safety net is gone. You can still decide to take the jump and enjoy the thrill but depending on the results, you could end up paying the price OR reaping the benefits of a thrilling, exciting experience. It's all up to you.

You will be responsible for identifying what needs to be done in your life, understanding how to do what needs to be done, doing it, and living with the consequences. However things turn out, you are the one who will ultimately get the pleasure or the pain for the decisions you make going forward. In most cases, there will not be someone else to blame or to bail you out if something goes wrong. It is all up to you.

YOU are responsible for making sure you have enough money in the bank to cover expenses until the next paycheck. YOU are responsible for how much you are spending. YOU are responsible for making sure your bills get paid on-time. Bounce a check, overdraw your account, or forget to pay your utility bill? There will be a consequence, most likely in the form of fees and other financial penalties. "Oops I forgot" will not get you out of the problem. YOU are responsible for keeping your affairs in order. If you don't, no one will do it for you.

Seem basic enough? Yes, but for someone who has lived all their life being controlled (in varying degrees) by someone else, accountability can be a bit overwhelming at first. But that is O.K. It is unrealistic for anyone to expect a young person venturing out in the world for the first time to just settle in and be accountable and responsible for everything without some degree of shock about all this freedom. It is an overwhelming experience at first. But you must accept it.

While you will find accountability permeating every aspect of your independent, self-sufficient adult life, you will really feel it in your work life…in the first year of your first real job. Of all the lessons your first year in a job will teach you, accountability may be the hardest to learn and accept. Even some employees who have worked for many years struggle with it.

The concept of accountability at work is that if something is expected of you, you will follow through and deliver. You are accountable for the work. YOU and no one else. If not, you may develop a reputation as one who does not keep his/her word, does not care about the needs of other co-workers, and cannot be counted on to deliver.

In school, it was easy to say "Sorry, I did not get it done" when you missed an assignment or a deadline. Or if you did not feel like going to class one day, no big deal. No one would be at risk of losing a job as a result of your inaction. But now the risks are greater. You could be in a position where not meeting your accountability could negatively impact others.

Let's say that you have been planning an event at a large annual conference where your company will be one of the featured organizations. Your company is sponsoring everything – breakfasts, dinners, featured speakers, even a large booth adorned with your company's logo and name. Planning the event has been very stressful, and you decide you just cannot deal with it any more. Even though the conference is tomorrow, you decide that you will just go home and let someone else figure out the rest of the details for your events. It is easier on you this way.

But no one else figures it out, and on the day of the conference, it is too late to limit the damage you have caused by walking away from your accountability. Your company's name is on everything at the conference, but the events you were accountable for (but dropped and left for someone else to figure out) are a complete disaster. Your company looks very bad in the eyes of thousands of conference attendees and everyone at the conference from your company is embarrassed. The person most damaged by the entire situation is not you, but your boss...the person who depended on you to deliver. His or her boss is now angry, and the boss's boss is angry, and as a result of your failure, it does not look good for your boss.

What can you do at this point? Nothing. The damage is done. But if you did not care at the time you dropped everything and went home, chances are you do not care now. You may not even view yourself as having any accountability for what did or did not happen. After all, someone else should have picked up where you left off.

But you DO have accountability. When you fail to deliver as promised, the person you let down is not going to care that you "just could not deal with it" or you "did not know" or that you "forgot but you are sorry." All they know is that you did not deliver.

You may think "I would not dream of missing my accountabilities for a large project such as this. You would have to be crazy not to see the ramifications of just leaving like that!" Granted, this is an extreme example, but accountability is not limited to large, complex projects. Accountability can show up in the day-to-day aspects of your job when someone asks you to make a call to a client or draft a proposal for them by a certain time. They are expecting you to complete the task or request. You are accountable for the work they have given you. Failing to meet your accountability in even simple situations like these could lead to greater problems.

For example, one morning your boss asks you to call a particular client by the end of the day and find out when the deadline is for your company to bid on a project. No problem, just a simple call. You have some other things to do, though, so instead of making the call immediately, you take care of some other things. These take more time than expected and by the time you are done, it is time to leave for the day. No problem, you think. I will make that call tomorrow. Tomorrow comes, and after a few other tasks are completed, you make the call. You find out that the deadline for submitting bids on the project was 5:00 PM the previous day. It is too late for your company to bid on a project that could have been worth millions…all because you didn't make a simple phone call as asked.

When you fail to meet your accountability, the person you failed may or may not say anything to you about it, but do not think they do not care. Following is a table which outlines some frequently used excuses about why someone did not deliver and what their boss/client may be thinking but not saying:

EXCUSE	CLIENT'S THOUGHT
"Accounting hasn't called back with the information."	Can you CALL them and ASK when we can expect it?
"I could not get to it."	Why not? You knew this was important.
"Something came up."	You should have told me. Unless it was an emergency, I was expecting you to deliver. In fact, I still am.
"It is not my fault."	Yes it is. I asked you to do it and it did not get done.
"It is not my job."	Yes it is. It became your job the minute I asked you to do it.
"I did not know how so I have not done it yet."	Could you not have asked or found someone who did know how?

Obviously, if an emergency comes up (a REAL emergency, involving things like pain, blood and death), no one is going to fault you for missing your accountability in that particular instance. But short of that, you are now expected to deliver results on whatever is assigned to you, no matter what. If you continually fail to meet your accountabilities, your value to your boss and to the business is greatly diminished. How can your boss give you a big project to handle if he or she has doubts about your willingness to follow through on all the details? Why should your supervisor put you in a high responsibility position if he or she has seen you cut and run when situations became stressful? Why would a project manager want you on his or her team if it is thought that you will spend more time thinking up excuses about why you could not deliver on-time than actually doing the work? They cannot, they should not and they would not. Will employers keep and promote employees who do not understand accountability? The answer most of the time is "no."

3.2 The First Year Emotional Curve

B ased on my own experience and those of others, it is reasonable to propose that your first year will follow a predictable emotional pattern. Yours may vary by a few months here and there, but the milestone events should be the same. For the first several months, you will be in the honeymoon period. EVERY-THING will be good with you. People will be friendly, the expectations of you will be low (because you are new and have not been in the job that long) and your 'plate' of responsibilities and obligations will be light. Your world will feel quite manageable from a work perspective.

Then, something will happen that will shatter the nirvana-type existence you have been living. You may start to see your 'to do' list fill with projects and feel more pressure from co-workers to provide assistance. You may make a very public, very obvious mistake. Or, you may begin dealing with complex issues much sooner than you expected. All of these events can increase your level of anxiety and stress and you may begin to feel overwhelmed. You may want to run away…literally. You may start to think, "Am I in the right job, the right company, or do I need to go back to school?" You may just want to go home, lock the door and be alone. Or you may feel the need to call every person on your speed dial for comfort.

Is this a warning sign that things, and you, are falling apart? No. In fact, it is a good omen. It indicates that you are being seen as a contributor instead of just a new employee straight from campus. When more responsibility comes your way, it means you are settling in and are starting to see the real world of work. Assuming you decide not to let this traumatic experience shut you down, you should start to see that you are moving forward professionally. As you begin to take on new responsibilities AND complete them, you will feel your confidence grow and you will start to see that you can succeed and contribute. Things that overwhelmed you in the early part of your first year may not seem as daunting now that you are taking on increasingly difficult situations and seeing them through to completion.

As the remainder of your first year winds down, you will be able to look back and see how far you have come. You may have one or two missteps along the way, but overall you should recognize your progress and give yourself credit for your success. You may want to consider keeping a journal to capture the highs and lows during your first year of your new job. Aside from being an interesting record for posterity, this history of your first year will enable you to look back and see the progress you have made. It will also serve as a helpful record during whatever type of performance evaluation you may receive.

When things are going a little rough, your journal will provide a broader perspective on your time to date, other than just the bad day or week you are having. It is easy to dwell on the negative and feel as if you are just spinning your wheels and not going anywhere. That is when the journal will be useful.

It can show that overall, you are doing O.K. Some of the items you noted in the early part of the year will cause you to realize there are many things you do not worry about any more, as well as many situations you now know how to handle. Some items may even make you laugh, depending on how you handled them at that time. It is a good exercise and it is something you can do on your own to get a little positive reinforcement in case feedback from your manager is not immediately forthcoming. We all need something that shows us that we are making forward progress, especially during the first year of our first real job.

3.3 *Your Hassle Factor*

About five years ago, my wife and I bought a new car to replace my aging college jalopy. We used every resource we had to bring the price down to where we could afford it: credit card points you could apply to vehicles, an employee discount through my company, trade in of the old car, and a little bit of cash we raised picking up cans by the side of the road (O.K., maybe the last part was made up, but we did use everything else). By nature we are not extravagant spenders, but for this purchase, we went all out. Leather seats, all the bells and whistles, even the flashy red paint that was limited to the high end model. We planned on making this car last for awhile, so we were O.K. with the expense. For about four years, the car ran great and we really enjoyed how it handled and rode. The gas mileage was good and because it was a six cylinder, it had plenty of power when it was needed. Our car was our friend.

Somewhere around Year Five, however, the friendship started to go south in a hurry. The water pump failed, spraying coolant all over the engine and requiring a complete change of belts. Two (yes, two) batteries died and one came close to exploding, according to the service guy who seemed a bit nervous as he removed it from the car. Strange noises came from the wheel well, making us wonder if it was something minor or if we would soon see our left front wheel waving to us from the other lane. Then, just after fixing yet another coolant leak, which caused us to keep a close eye on the coolant level every other day, the topper: complete and total engine failure due to a fully drained battery and dead alternator at four thousand feet of elevation on a stretch of a mountain road where there was absolutely no cell service. It is one thing to be fuming mad that you were going to incur yet ANOTHER repair bill on a car that you would love to push off a cliff. It is a completely different experience to be fuming AND trying to coast a two-ton rolling chunk of metal down a mountain with no power steering or power brakes.

We no longer own this car. It was sold for a few magic beans and its blue book value approximately two weeks after this little experience. Why, you ask? An alternator is a relatively cheap repair compared to replacing the whole car, isn't it? Weren't the leather seats still soft and comfortable? Didn't the six cylinder engine still kick out enough power and give you decent gas mileage? Did the gadgets still work? Yes to all of it, but the key factor was…I could no longer trust it. Its hassle factor became too high.

I see the same concept of 'hassle factor' come into play when managers describe employees who contribute a significant amount through their jobs but require more than the average amount of attention. Such as:

- The sales employee who consistently beats his sales numbers but treats fellow employees so poorly that people quit the company or leave the department;
- The graphic design employee who produces phenomenally creative work but cannot be counted on to deliver the completed project by the deadline;
- The project manager who is the best in the company but spends at least an hour a week in her

supervisor's office complaining about her pay and asking for a promotion;

- The programmer who produces fast, efficient results but has a temper that makes clients reluctant to work with him on projects.

These examples illustrate some of the ways an employee can reduce the value of their contribution to their employer and more importantly, their manager, by having a high hassle factor. Managers may tolerate employees who do tremendous jobs but create headaches for them, but only under certain conditions.

What are these conditions? Imagine a balancing scale. One tray holds the contributions of the employee and the other tray holds the frustrations or extra work a "high hassle factor" employee creates for his or her manager. As long as the employee's contribution side is outweighing or equal to the frustrations side, the manager will most likely put up with the employee's problematic behavior. But should the scale begin to tip the other way, it is likely the manager will reach the end of his or her patience and either address the issue through discipline or move the employee out of the organization.

High hassle factor employees create problems for everyone. They can create resentment among other employees in the workplace. These 'low hassle factor' employees are working hard and not causing trouble, but they do not see their boss spending any extra time with them. They may also wonder if they would receive the same preferential treatment if they hit a rough patch in their job performance and needed the boss to be patient while they worked things out.

High hassle factor employees cause problems for managers, too. The manager's dilemma is whether to try and mold the employee into shape, hoping the employee will get over whatever problematic behaviors are exhibited, or just keep cleaning up the messes?

So what do we do about it? We (employees) do not do anything about it. That is why managers get paid the big bucks – to handle headaches like this. But you can serve yourself well by making sure you understand your own 'hassle factor,' or those things that could create a hassle factor for your boss, and try to keep your 'factor' as low as possible.

For this exercise, you will need to step back and take an honest look at yourself and say, do I have any habits or behaviors that could potentially grow into hassle factors for my manager or supervisor? As with other guidance I have given you throughout this book, feedback from others who know you well would be of tremendous benefit as it is difficult to be objective about ourselves. Some areas you may be able to assess on your own, however, are:

- Are you chronically late? If so, could this lateness impact your work in any way? Would people know when they could expect your work to get done?
- Do you handle accountability well or do you over-commit and under-deliver on your obligations and responsibilities? If the latter, it is not a question of when your work would get done, it is a question of

whether it would get done at all! Not something a manager wants to worry about from an employee for very long.

- Do you keep your emotions in check when dealing with other people in difficult situations, or do you take the opportunity to prove the saying "Never back down from a fight?" Will your boss need to go behind you to manage the damage to your department or your company's reputation as a result of your confrontations?

What is the #1 hassle factor of all time? In my experience, the hands-down winner is the chronic complainer. Let's put this into context, however. Problems do crop up in the workplace and the only way a manager knows about many of them is if someone complains about them. Obviously, a manager cannot fix what he or she does not know about. The most effective complaints, however, are followed up with "instead, could we try it this way?" or "what might work differently is..." I personally love these complaints because I find out about the problem AND learn a possible solution.

But when the high hassle factor complainer shows up, they usually complain about nothing specific (they do not have a particular problem but they are not happy and they want you to know it) or they have a specific, lengthy complaint but have no idea or recommendation for how to resolve it. They also seem to have a need to perpetually bring problems/complaints of every shape and size to the manager's door.

If you have a complaint or problem, DO bring it to your manager for discussion, but include at least a general suggestion on how the situation could be remedied. Otherwise, it is as if you just vomited on your manager and walked away – you feel better but they have a mess on their hands. I do not particularly care for people doing that to me, and I am thinking your manager will not be fond of it, either.

If you cannot think of a solution to your problem, it may be that you do not have a true complaint. You may just need to whine. Work problems need to be shared with your manager; whines should be shared with friends. But if you feel the need to behave like the chronic complainer, do so at your own peril. As the saying goes, "chronic complaining is like a car alarm – people start tuning it out after awhile." Your boss may begin dismissing your opinions and completely tune you out…just like we ignore car alarms.

3.4 This Is Not Reality TV

Unless you have been wrapped up in a really, really LONG book for the past several years, you have seen the reality TV craze explode. The pioneer in this genre is a show where a group of very diverse individuals are placed in some God-forsaken location far away from civilization and forced to 'survive' until the end of the show. Of course, survival in this context not only means meeting basic food and water needs and avoiding bugs and other things that could...well...kill you. Oh, no. It also means surviving the tribal council meetings where you could get voted off the show, which would cause you to lose your chance to win a million bucks.

One of the ways that the winners survive is by playing relationship games amongst their fellow tribe members; making sure more votes are cast for someone else than for them at tribal council. One week you may see that Mary is aligned to Sally, Joe and Bob. The next week, however, she'll change alliances to Jimmy, Stan and Paula because Sally got voted off, so there is one less ally and quite frankly, it does not make much sense to stay aligned with Joe and Bob. Joe has starting walking around naked and Bob seems to be spending a lot of his time alone with some imaginary friend he talks to in the bushes. Of course, Mary then gets voted off at the next tribal council because the imaginary friend Bob was talking to was actually his new alliance of Jimmy, Stan and Paula hiding in the bushes deciding whether to vote Mary or Joe off. So, she leaves the game and yes, Joe is still in the game.

Naked…but still in the game.

Any time you put people together in a group, you will see subgroups start to form. The larger the group, the more likely this phenomenon will occur, but even in small groups you may see folks start to cluster and form their own subgroups or cliques. Since you are not that far removed from the cliquish high school years, you probably have a good idea what I am talking about. These sub-groups can form along many lines — age, race, gender, previous familiarity, looks, etc. Whatever makes people feel a common bond will bring them together and either include, or exclude, you.

Whenever these situations occur, you may find yourself in a situation not unlike being a contestant on a reality TV show: feeling like you have to play games to survive. As the 'fresh out of school college grad,' you are the new kid on the block. You do not know yet who is credible and who is not. The smiling faces and helpful words being offered by your new co-workers are likely meant in the most innocent, meaningful, useful way, but allow me to provide a few things to consider.

Hopefully, your co-workers will not have imaginary friends or walk around naked, but there may be some folks who like to play the alliance game and would LOVE for you to join their team. Only in these situations, you run the risk of creating headaches for yourself that will not help your career or your job satisfaction. These alliances typically direct their efforts toward at least one of three targets:

The boss: Managers get slightly higher pay for putting up with some of the most bizarre and frustrating things people can dream up. An alliance can target the boss for any reason; appearance, age, work style, or maybe just because he or she is the boss. When the boss is the target of an alliance, there are generally two or three employees who have been royally ticked off and in return, they want to make that person's life miserable. For example, these employees may purposely interact with the boss as little as possible and when they have to interact, the tone of their voice and the look in their eyes express a cold dislike. Or maybe when a problem comes up, they subtly use it as a public opportunity to make the boss look incompetent or portray him/her as the cause of the problem. The boss is the enemy, and the alliance wants it to be known.

The company: Some folks, no matter how well they are treated by a company, simply like to complain about it. Like many things in life, it is more fun to complain with other people than by yourself. Alliances will search around until they find kindred complaining spirits who share the similar negative views of the company and try to pull them into their group. Then, they will form a small circle, get some coffee and donuts and start griping about the company, often at the expense of anything productive getting done.

Other employees: Employees who consistently perform their jobs well are sometimes targeted by alliances because their performance makes the employees in the alliance look bad. There is no tolerance for an employee who can produce as much work as all the members of the alliance combined! Or there could be other reasons that a group of employees want another employee/group of employees to have a difficult time of it...like their age or the color of their skin. You can use your imagination as to the reasons. Sometimes the retaliation by the alliance is quite overt but often it is more subtle; gossip intended to make the employee look bad, actions to slow down something this employee needs to do their job, or actions that make the employee feel unwelcome. As long as the targeted employee looks bad or is miserable, the alliance has achieved its objective.

These alliances run on emotion, not on fact, and the negativity of their actions poisons the workplace. You are paid to do a job. Part of doing your job implies being fair and objective and working from fact, not emotion, with your co-workers and your manager. If you find yourself drawn to the opportunities alliances offer for creating tension and chaos based on negativity, be forewarned. As a new employee, you have a very limited supply of political capital — that is, the amount of unproductive, negative behavior that will be tolerated before your manager's patience with you runs out. You may think that by participating in an alliance you are building an effective working relationship with your co-workers. You are not.

Instead, you are creating a problem for yourself that the manager will need to address. He/she may address it at the first available opportunity by either moving you out of the department, or maybe even out of the company. Remember, you are still relatively new and while you may have arrived with a high amount of potential, you reduce that potential by becoming someone the boss needs to be wary of, instead of a contributing employee who he or she can depend on to do the right things for the right reasons. Once you are perceived as being anything other than unbiased, your credibility is dirtied a bit in the eyes of your boss, even if the perception is wrong.

Your best course of action is to keep interactions light with those who appear to want to drag you into some type of alliance. If you feel as if you are being pressured to take sides on an issue or behave in a manner that your logic and objectivity would otherwise caution you against, back away. How can you know when you may be drifting into one of these situations?

Buried deep within your brain is a little red flag. It has been there since the day you were born, and your body has been in tune with it for many years. It starts waving when you encounter things that are not quite right or appear different than what was expected.

For example, if you start the shower and let it run for a few minutes but you still have no hot water, your red flag should start waving. Something is wrong. You expected hot water and you are only getting cold water. If you are driving down the street and your car coughs and dies, your red flag should start waving. You likely were not expecting the car to die, so something must be wrong. Your red flag can help you see when there may be more to a situation than meets the eye. If faced with a situation where the facts you observe are not consistent with what you are feeling pressured to do, your red flag is waving. You should avoid involvement with whatever the situation may be.

If someone or a group is pressuring you to act one way but you refuse, could this refusal make your future interactions with them difficult? Yes. Making a choice to go against group pressure for the right reasons never comes without some type of pain. But it is the right thing to do, and it is easier to live with decisions you make for the right reasons.

Someone who considers all facts and facets of a situation before deciding on his or her course of action may sometimes stand alone in their desire to do the right thing. But they become a testimony to the value of strong character and an inspiration to others who may need a role model to show them it is O.K. to do the right thing. A willingness to live by a standard of professional behavior grounded in fact, instead of influenced by the emotions of others, is a solid stone to place in your career foundation so early in your professional life. Many difficult decisions await you in the future, but committing to do the right things for the right reasons now makes those future decisions much easier.

3.5 I did WHAT Last Night?

Question: Which of these places and events is considered part of your workplace?

A. Happy hour at the neighborhood bar
B. Thursday night ballgame after work
C. Weekend pool parties with co-workers

A, B, or C? All? None of the above?

Unless the company is sponsoring one of the events, none of these are. It is not unreasonable, though, that you could attend these or similar events with people from work since they are the people you spend the most time with each week. Socializing outside of work is a good way to bond and build relationships with your co-workers. But while your employer does not have any say over what you do or how you behave towards co-workers in these situations, you need to be aware of how off-the-job activities with co-workers can bleed back over into your work environment.

For example, two female company recruiters were invited to dinner by some recent campus hires prior to the company's orientation session. The dinner was not paid for by the company, it was just a group of employees going out to eat. Over the course of the evening (and several drinks later), one of the newly hired males became increasingly open about how he felt about one of the female recruiter's looks, describing her as a "very pretty lady" and "someone I would like to get to know better."

She handled it well by politely saying "thanks" but she would prefer to be viewed in a professional light and keep their interactions as such. Though the recruiter kept her personal opinions about this individual to herself going forward, others within earshot at the table saw this interaction and were not as discrete. The female employees nicknamed him 'Slick' and in my opinion, he was never perceived as being a serious contributor from that point on...just a player trying to get a date.

A peer of mine went out for appetizers with a group of people from work, and included in the group was a relatively new employee who thought everyone would appreciate hearing his comments and jokes about various females at their company. When one of the more experienced employees at the table asked him if these were the type of comments they should expect to hear from him if he ever became a manager in the company, he became very quiet.

Because of that event, a seed of concern was planted with my peer and others at the table about how this individual would view and treat female employees in the workplace. Would female employees be peers or potential playmates to him? He obviously was not feeling the need to single out male employees for personal scrutiny and ridicule. Female employees, though, appeared to deserve this 'special' treatment in his eyes. If he was ever promoted into a role that included managing people, would he utilize that power in a way demeaning to women? And how would he treat others who looked differently from him? A bevy of concerns arose from just one interaction.

My personal favorite, though, was 'The Dancer.' She was a new hire from a high-end MBA program who, over the course of the interview process and her first few weeks on the job, was p3: polished, professional and poised. Outside of work, though, a strange transformation occurred when she and her co-workers would hit the club scene on the weekends. A little alcohol and some loud dance music helped her relax out of her p3 persona to 'The Dancer,' an alter ego who enjoyed demonstrating extremely sensual dance moves; practicing the visual seduction of any and all men who happened to be nearby.

Is it illegal to dance? No, at least not where I grew up. But it does beg the question about what type of image the employee, no matter how confident or skilled, would present to a customer or client in situations where alcohol and good times may both be flowing freely. Many business functions, especially in the evening, can be held in an atmosphere that is more social and relaxed than the business environment where she so effectively demonstrated the p3 persona. How would she behave? The question lingered.

These are some obvious faux paus, and you may be thinking "I'd never do things like this so I must be O.K. on this topic." "I made it through the interviews and social mixers," you say, "and I got the job. Why do I need to worry about this?" But are there any other "socially embarrassing" behaviors you tend to exhibit from time-to-time that you need to be aware of and potentially control?

In an interview setting, people are generally on their best behavior as they know they are being evaluated. But don't think that once you are in your new job, your employer stops evaluating your behavior. Company events, and even informal gatherings where company employees are present, can be valuable for expanding your network of contacts, but they can also damage your image if you are not careful.

We can sometimes be blind to personal behaviors that could create problems for us in a work group or team setting. These could be behaviors you exhibit in particular situations such as when you are drinking alcohol, feeling stress, or are uncomfortable in a group setting. The behaviors that you exhibit in these situations may not be indicative of how you really are, but people observe them and begin forming assumptions about you.

The assumptions or opinions people form about you, accurate or not, are hard to overcome. Remember, elephants and the people who can affect your career have very good memories. If you are not sure whether you exhibit some potentially "embarrassing" behaviors, seek out acquaintances that will give you honest feedback and ask them if there are any behaviors they have noticed that make them uncomfortable. Try to understand when you exhibit these behaviors, what may cause the behaviors to occur, and make an effort to keep the behaviors from occurring in the future.

None of us is perfect, and from time-to-time we all do things we wish we could go back and undo. But your professional life does not offer you many second chances to correct mistakes, especially ones that cause people to form opinions about you. Being open to feedback and willing to change problematic behaviors in the present will help you avoid embarrassing situations in the future that could derail your ability to show your true potential.

3.6 Teambuilding: Just the Two of Us

Some nights I have to drag myself into bed, physically exhausted from the drain of a long work day, the tedium of a big city commute, and the limitless energy of a toddler. My mind, however, is still wide awake, racing with thoughts of the day with no intention of letting me rest. So with the hope of finding something that will gently numb my brain into a peaceful slumber, I usually turn on the TV and start surfing, careful to avoid football games or anything else that will make my adrenaline rush so late in the evening. If I'm lucky, I will stumble across one of those plot deprived movies from the 1970's where all the main characters miraculously get all their problems solved and everyone smiles and cheers, straight through the closing credits. Those movies bore me right to sleep.

One night, I was out in TV land searching for my mental sleeping pill when I stumbled onto the perfect candidate: a TV movie where the main characters met, fell in love, and finally married, at work! It was so touching! The main work floor was the sanctuary, the coffee room was the reception hall, and the boss presided over the ceremony as lines of teary-eyed co-workers peeked wistfully over their cubes to catch a glimpse of the lucky couple. A match made in heaven.

I was asleep in ten minutes.

Why do I bring this up? Although I am all for people falling in love, you need to be aware of a potential problem in your new work life you may not have considered: dating your co-workers. When you were in school, you may have had a fairly active social life. It is also reasonable to assume that included in that social life were several (or a few, or more than you care to count) romantic, dating-type relationships. You probably had very few limitations around with whom you became romantically involved. Even then, the limitations were mainly peer related (i.e. your friends thought he was a jerk) or societal (do not date your sister...please). Now that you are moving into a workplace, you will have more limitations on your romantic relationships to consider, either from your employer's rules or by the difficulties dating in the workplace can cause you personally.

Because you may meet and get to know many of your co-workers, it is reasonable to believe that you may find someone in whom you will have more than just a passing interest. The majority of relationships you have in your life occur with people you spend a substantial amount of time with in some capacity. Think back to high school. Who did you date? People you went to school with, people you went to church with, etc. You saw them the most and had more opportunities to spend time with them, and thus form some type of bond. This same situation carried over to college with the students in your classes, your dorm and your social organizations. Your new work life will offer these same social opportunities, as well.

You spend at least eight hours a day and five days a week confined in the same building with the same group of people. It is only reasonable that you will get to know a few of them, and these are not just any people. These are folks who found the same things appealing about your employer or organization as you did when you were thinking about taking the job. You may have likes and dislikes that are very similar, too, making the personal attraction that much stronger.

"Just what is wrong with this," you ask? "Isn't work about working as a team?" Well, yes, but there are cautions around just how broadly you can define "team." I mentioned two limitations above that you could encounter: your employer's rules and personal difficulties for you.

The first, your employer's rules, has to do with whether companies expressly state that you cannot become romantically involved with your co-workers. This practice varies widely across organizations, with some prohibiting it and others not addressing it at all. If there is no rule about dating your co-workers, you are free to date as you'd like. But if there is a policy that forbids you from dating your co-workers, you will need to be aware of that and to follow it.

Why do companies even have policies around dating? Companies often put these limitations in place because romantic relationships can have negative effects on a team or a work group. Work is mainly a logical endeavor: something needs doing, you do it, you get paid; something else needs doing, you do it, too, and you get paid. There is no emotion involved with the professional relationship. Personal relationships, however, are largely based on emotion, both the good AND the bad. When the relationship is going well, co-workers who are dating appear happy and content.

But when things go bad, these same two co-workers are anything but happy and content and their co-workers know it. Group tension may become high, alliances can form, and heated arguments can flare up between the two romantically-involved employees. Companies know this, and since romantic relationships do not have anything to do with the product or service a company or organization produces or provides, many employers simply prohibit employee dating altogether. It is not worth the hassle.

What happens if you meet your soul mate but your company prohibits employee dating? If you decide to move forward with a relationship, you could be disciplined or asked to leave the company if the relationship is discovered. After all, you did violate a rule.

How do you find out whether your company prohibits dating? I do NOT recommend walking into your boss's office during your first year simply for the purpose of asking whether you can date your co-workers. One boss may view this as a warning sign. Another boss may think you are trying to ask him or her out. You do not want either of these situations. Instead, look at your employee handbook or at your organization's posted policies. If there is a policy in place, it should be clearly posted and easy to find. At the very least, ask your HR person whether the company or organization has limitations on employee dating.

But what if your company does not prohibit employees from having relationships? Technically, you are free to move ahead as you see fit, just be aware of the downside if the relationship ends, because your work life could get a bit uncomfortable. If you worked closely with this person or depended on them for something to get your job done, how are you going to handle that now? You still have to get your job done and so do they, regardless of your situation.

In an earlier section, we discussed how to build an effective working relationship with a co-worker who may not have you at the top of their 'favorite person' list. But that situation was not personal. This is. You know why you are not getting along; they hate you. The solution is not as easy as finding a way to work together. Oh, no. You would need to psychoanalyze the entire personal relationship and find the cause of the problem in that relationship before you could even begin to solve the work relationship.

Even if the romantic relationship is working great, issues can arise that create problems for you and for your partner in the workplace. For example, how will your co-workers perceive you in light of your relationship? Are you more interested in romance than the equipment you are supposed to be inspecting? Are you spending too much time hanging around your new found love's desk or cube instead of doing your share of the work? Is your furious typing work-related or are you instant messaging your plans for the weekend to your sweetheart? Your co-workers may start to question some of your actions and are likely to share these concerns with your boss.

With the topics we have covered up to this point, I have tried to provide you with practical guidance about how to handle various situations. On this topic, however, that would be a waste of time because relationships are all about emotion, not logic. As you probably know, emotions win out over logic when love is the topic on the table. Emotions can take us to the heights of ecstasy one minute, and then pull us through the fires of hell the next. For all the grief emotions cause us, we long for the contentment they give us when we find the right match with someone else. I understand that, and I am not going to fool myself by thinking that my logic could ever take precedent over your emotion when it comes to love.

That said, all I can do is what I did in this chapter: discuss the "legality" and the downside of dating in the workplace so that you are more aware of the risks and limitations. So unless your company expressly prohibits dating in the workplace, it is ultimately your decision whether or not to date your co-workers. I can argue both sides of the issue; I have seen these relationships work and seen them fail. All things considered, I have to defer to the guidance provided by an old Scottish proverb that says: "Be happy while you are living, for you are a long time dead." You may infer whatever you like about my position on this matter.

Choose well...and good luck.

3.7 Money - YOUR Money

Money, money, money. It makes the world go 'round. It is why we work, why we went to school (to get more money when we did start working), and if you listen to the experts, it is one of the bigger things we worry about. Money plays a big part in our lives whether we like it or not. After all, if we did not need this little thing called a 'paycheck,' many of us would probably be doing something other than getting up early, fighting traffic, and sitting through boring meetings each day. But we DO need money to survive. We have to pay bills, buy groceries, and keep the government running, and money helps us meet these needs.

I realize you have had experience managing your own small budget while you have been in school. This was probably a mish mash of income from parents, guardians, grandparents, loans and a part-time job. I will also surmise it was just enough to pay your limited expenses and still have enough to party on the weekend and make it to Cozumel in the spring. Otherwise, you probably had very little extra spending money. For most of us, the college years were a little lean. But now that we are working, WOW! Look at the size of that paycheck! We make more money in a week than we used to make in a MONTH! We are RICH! No more worries for us. We are SET. Hey, let's go shopping and maybe buy a new car!

Stop. You may not have as much extra money as you think by the time you have accounted for all the expenses related to being on your own. With a full-time job, you will be receiving more 'disposable' income in one paycheck than you did in several months of school, but you will also have more expenses, and who is responsible for paying those? You are. Remember our talk about "accountability?" You have accountability for managing your money from the first day you begin working. Financial matters are much more complex as a working adult and you will find that your money will not go as far as you think.

For example, a new single graduate living in a metro area with a starting salary of $38,000 per year will have monthly income and expenses similar to the following:

Monthly Gross Pay	**$ 3,166.67**
Less:	
Federal Withholding Tax	$ (335.00)
Social Security Tax	$ (180.32)
Medicare Tax	$ (42.17)
State Income Tax (6%)	$ (133.67)
Employee Benefit Premiums (pre-tax)	$ (100.00)
401K Savings (5% of pay)	$ (158.33)
Net Take Home Pay	**$ 2,217.18**
Less:	
Automobile Gas	$ (100.00)
Automobile Insurance	$ (50.00)
Automobile Maintenance	$ (20.00)
Cable	$ (50.00)
Cell Phone	$ (40.00)
Clothing	$ (100.00)
Electricity	$ (100.00)
Natural Gas	$ (25.00)
Telephone	$ (50.00)
Groceries/Household	$ (150.00)
Rent	$ (1,100.00)
Renters Insurance	$ (10.00)

Eating out four $20 meals/month	$ (80.00)
Miscellaneous Spending	$ (100.00)
Net Remaining	**$ 242.18**

There isn't much left over after paying the bills, is there? Our above example does not even include such payments as car loans, credit card payments, student loans, etc., which would take that remaining balance down even lower. Once you are out on your own, you need to figure out how much money you need to SURVIVE and manage your available funds to meet those needs.

What does managing your money have to do with working? More than you think. Like it or not, your financial health and limitations play a role in how satisfied you are with your life and your job. I am NOT saying that your happiness will be directly related to your financial status. What I am saying, however, is that how you manage your finances when you are first starting out can affect your level of satisfaction with your life circumstances. To be balanced, your job should be the means by which you support the basic needs and activities of your life. What we want to AVOID is a situation where your job can barely support your basic needs because of overaggressive spending. This is what we will call a "subsistence existence." I will explain.

Let's look at the person living on the budget we just exampled, Mr. Twister. He decides that since he has just graduated and started his new job, the time is right to get a sportier car than the two year old fuel-efficient car he has been driving. At the end of the deal, Mr. Twister ends up with a brand-spanking new Twistermobile with a monthly payment of $200. Not bad, and as you can see, he can afford this payment as long as he stays within his budget. Things look O.K. so far.

Well, when you have a new car like Mr. Twister, you may decide that you need a few additional outfits and of course, a trip to the beach to show off the sunroof. It is just a weekend trip, of course, since he does not have vacation yet at his new job. Paying cash? Oh, no. We are going to CHARGE all this on his new credit card because we get frequent flyer miles...and that is a good deal, right? So, Mr. T charges up about $600 in total expenses on his card and we are good to go. The problem is that Mr. T continues to charge little things here and there for the next six months because he does not have enough cash in his budget to support his spending. He is scraping together just enough to cover the minimum monthly payment on his credit card. But remember, he's getting frequent flyer miles so the more he charges, the better the deal!

Six months after graduation, Mr. Twister is still having a blast and his job is rolling along just fine. When he arrives home one evening, he finds a letter from his student loan company with a payment booklet inside. Mr. Twister has just learned that for the next 25 years, he is going to be paying $193 month at 6% interest on the $30,000 in student loans he incurred while in college. AND, his latest credit statement shows he owes close to $3,000 on his credit card and he now has a MINIMUM payment each month of $75. That is not including anything to bring the balance on the card down! He's just paying interest. In six months he has gone from having an extra $242 each month to being in the hole by $226, which will not change for many years without drastic action.

Where will the extra money come from to cover this gap? Can he get a raise? He'll probably get an annual raise when he hits one year of service, but at most, he shouldn't expect more than around a 5% increase in his salary. This would allow him to bring home an extra $110 a month (approximately) but he'll still be in the hole by around $116, assuming his rent does not go up, his utilities do not increase, etc. So where else could the money come from?

He'll have to start taking it from his basic living expenses. Maybe he can drop the extra cable channels, or buy fewer clothes. Or maybe he can try taking public transportation instead of his new car to save on gas money. Or maybe he can start taking his lunch to work instead of eating out each day with his friends. There are multiple options, but all will require a reduction in his basic spending habits. As a result, he no longer looks at his job as the source of money for both living and enjoying life. Instead, he is enslaved to his paycheck.

Because of his financial straits in the present, he has severe restrictions on what he can do in the future. What if he wants to go back to school? How will he cover his expenses? Borrow more money? He could, but he would be borrowing money to service his credit card balance and pay his car payment. That is not a good arrangement because you are using debt to pay off debt. Luckily his student loan payment will stop when he returns to school, but it will continue to accumulate interest on the unpaid balance. It will not just go away because he returned to school.

Mr. Twister used to feel in control as he had a job he liked and a life he enjoyed. Now he sees his job as a necessary evil and as something he must hold on to, no matter what. All because he spent more money than he made in the first few months of his first year working and did not recognize the problem until it all came due. Is this a drastic example? Not really.

I have had friends over the years in situations similar to this and they did not have many options for getting out of it. In fact, they just seemed to make it worse and worse. I have one friend who bought an expensive two door foreign sports car right out of school but had no furniture in his apartment except for a mattress, a TV and a card table. He could not afford anything else. Once he started seeing the credit card bills/student loans/etc. piling up, he had to declare bankruptcy...at 24 years of age. It does not take long to spend money you borrow, but it takes forever to pay it back...if you can ever pay it all back.

So what is the message here? It is to watch what you are spending your first year or two out of school. Seems like a basic message, but for whatever reason, so many of us just do not get it. There is nothing wrong with driving a slightly used car, living conservatively, or maybe waiting for a sale before buying new work clothes. You will eventually figure out what is worth the money and what is not and will be willing to sacrifice for the purchase. It takes time to gain this internal meter of value, but until you have it, every purchase will seem just as necessary as the next, and that is just not true.

Some other factors to keep in mind as you manage your new-found wealth follow.

LEAVING CAMPUS

Understand how frequently you get paid and how long that money may last. Companies pay on varying intervals: some are every two weeks, some twice a month, a few even monthly. The problem is that the fewer times per month you get paid, the bigger the net amount that goes into your bank account on payday. When you see this big balance in your account, you may think you have more than enough money to cover all your expenses and that you can spend, spend, spend as you see fit. But be careful. You have to make that money last until your next paycheck and it is very easy to nickel and dime yourself into running out of money well before you get paid again.

Now that you are out on your own, you do not have a lot of options to bridge any gaps in income. You may want to be fairly conservative during your first months until you understand how your bills are going to fall relative to your paychecks. Rent, likely your biggest expense, usually falls in the early part of the month. Utility bills, phone bills, car payments, insurances, etc., can be scattered throughout the month, leaving the end of the month as when you may see that bank account running dry.

Student loans may come into play at some point if you had to borrow money to get through school. Usually there is a six month deferral between when you graduate and when you start making payments on your loans. As most students graduate in the spring (not all, but most), this six month deferral period usually wraps up around the holidays about the time you are doling out huge hunks of cash for gifts, parties and trips home.

Understand the Impact of Credit on Your Finances. You may be inundated by offers for credit cards and "low" interest rates for items vendors say you absolutely cannot live without — such as new furniture and other household items — all paid on "deferred payment plans" and "no money down." Zero percent financing on new automobiles and similar high-dollar items may also tempt you. You will not have much trouble getting credit because you have tremendous earning potential in front of you and, unless you declared bankruptcy in college, your credit record should be fairly clean. Plus, businesses are finding that the best way to get their products out the door is to offer some very liberal financing to the masses and go with the odds that most people will meet their obligations and pay them off.

When companies are qualifying you for credit, however, they are not looking out for your well-being. They do not sit down and calculate whether the monthly payment you will incur will still permit you to pay your rent, your utilities, and buy yourself enough food to maintain a healthy lifestyle. Oh, no. Their calculation is based on the assumption that most of the money you have left out of your paycheck can and will be applied against whatever loan amount you choose to borrow from them. After the deal is done and the papers signed, they could really care less what happens to you. If you do not pay, they'll sell your loan account to some other company at a discount and let the other company worry about getting the money out of you.

Credit card companies will not only be thrilled when you open an account with them but will turn cartwheels if you start carrying a balance on the account and only pay the minimum amount each month. They can charge you an outrageous interest rate on the unpaid balance, usually around 21-22%. In other words, you would pay the credit card company about 22 cents for every dollar you owe on your credit card balance over the course of one year. Your spending and financial habits create a lucrative income stream for credit card companies and the like. They make about twice as much from you than they could investing their cash in a reasonable business venture. Why would they not want to extend you credit? You make them rich!

You COULD be a rebel and just pay everything in cash, but unfortunately in this day and age, you need a credit card to book flight reservations or rent a car. But that does not mean you need to carry a balance on your card. The safest strategy with credit cards is to pay off the balance each month as your statement arrives. Your credit card company may not like you as much as they first appeared to when they see you are not carrying big balances and paying hefty fees. But you will feel a lot better.

Watch Your Cash Burn and Spending Habits. Even if you are careful not to use a high-interest credit card to finance your day-to-day life, you will need to watch the little expenses here and there that can eat up more of your available income than you might think. Things like eating out for lunch and dinner, having drinks after work, and going to movies, plays and concerts can be relatively inexpensive amounts by themselves, but when you lump them all together in an average week or month, they pack quite a punch. The following table assumes a typical Monday through Friday spending pattern for someone working in an office job.

Monday Lunch	$ 7.59
Monday Dinner	$ 17.56
Tuesday Lunch	$ 7.59
ATM Withdrawal fee	$ 2.50
Tuesday Dinner	$ 5.73
Wednesday Lunch	$ 11.68
Wednesday Drinks	$ 14.23
ATM Withdrawal fee	$ 2.50
Thursday Lunch	$ 7.59
Thursday Evening Movie	$ 12.00
Friday Lunch	$ 13.22
ATM Withdrawal fee	$ 2.50
Friday Dinner	$ 18.67
	$ 123.36

This could vary one way or the other for you, but for a single person working a nine-to-five position in reasonably-sized metropolitan area, it is realistic. Multiplied by four weeks in a typical month; these areas alone could consume almost $500 of your monthly disposable income. That is no small number. You may be a person who packs a lunch, goes to matinee movies and uses a two-for-one coupon for dinners out and, if so, your expenses would obviously be lower. But this may not be far off from how your typical week could go if you do not monitor your expenses. Once your bank account is depleted, it is depleted until the next payday.

Take Advantage of the Benefits Offered By Your Company. Your job likely comes with benefits, and if so, you should use these benefits to their utmost advantage. Because of a company's size, you can get various financial and insurance products that can help you build wealth and minimize financial risks much more cheaply than you can on your own. Following is a narrative of a typical benefits package you will find with most companies and how each benefit can be helpful to you:

Health Insurance: If there was any other reason to work aside from a paycheck, it is the ability to get health insurance at a decent price. For someone who is young and probably relatively healthy, it may seem like a minor thing. In fact, you may even be tempted to pass on the insurance, take the money from your employer (if they permit that), and go find coverage on your own. Don't do it. The coverage with your employer is going to be a much better value than anything you could pay for yourself. Employers typically contribute some towards the cost of your monthly insurance premium (sometimes paying up to 80% of the bill). Outside of your company's plan, you will have to pay the full amount for any coverage and it probably will not cover near as much nor limit what you have to pay in the event of illness.

You generally see two types of plans offered by a company: Health Maintenance Organizations (HMOs) and general indemnity plans or something similar. With HMO's, you will pay a small amount towards whatever you are having done and the plan will pay for everything else. The limitation is that you can only go to certain doctors and hospitals that participate in the HMO network, or they will not pay anything. With general indemnity plans, you usually end up paying a percentage of the cost of whatever you are having done and the plan pays for the rest. Usually indemnity plans also require you to pay some costs before they will start to pay anything. This is called meeting your deductible. Once you meet your deductible and the medical plan starts paying, it will pay about 80% of the typical bill.

Most plans will limit what you have to pay out of your own pocket in any given year. They'll pay for everything after that until the next year begins.

Why is health insurance important? The biggest benefit to having medical insurance is that you limit what you will have to pay in the event you have a serious medical situation. You know as well as I do that you can walk into any doctor's office or any hospital in the country without insurance and they'll gladly do whatever you want them to. But you will ultimately have to pay all the bills, and they are not cheap. When my wife and I had our first child, we paid out about $1,000 towards the cost of her birth. When I saw the total bill later, insurance paid $6,500. Without insurance, we would have had to pull together $7,500 to cover our daughter's birth. While we would gladly pay any amount necessary to make sure her birth went well, it was nice not to have the bulk of that expense coming out of our pocket.

Dental Plans: Dental plans are obviously intended for dental-related issues (duh), and there is not a lot of variability among dental plans. You should find that your annual cleanings (you DO get your teeth cleaned twice a year, right?) are covered completely, which will save you money and hopefully prevent the need for more dental work. Should you need more involved dental work (crowns, bridges, fillings, etc.), your dental insurance will pay a portion of the costs related to these procedures, but not the full amount. As crowns can run $400 and up, dental insurance is another one of those insurances that will save you a little money short-term but will be a hedge against larger expenses if they come up later on.

LEAVING CAMPUS

Vision Plans: Most companies participate in programs where you can get discounts on eye exams and eyeglasses/contacts. Eye exams can run anywhere from $50 to $100. New glasses (including lenses) can be upwards of $250, depending on the type and style you purchase. Contact lenses, depending on the type, can run $20-30 a month. Since vision plans only cost you about $6 per pay check (at the most), you do save some money on vision related expenses in a typical year by using your vision plan.

Flexible Spending Accounts (FSAs): Flexible spending accounts are accounts that you can put money into that you can use for either medical expenses or child care. The biggest benefit is that the money comes out of your paycheck before taxes are deducted and thus lowers your taxable income AND gives you a little extra money to apply towards the expenses. For example, if I make $1000 a paycheck and have no other deductions taken out, my paycheck would look like this:

Weekly Gross Pay	**$ 1,000.00**
Federal Withholding	$ 159.52
Social Security	$ 62.00
Medicare	$ 14.50
State (6%)	$ 50.58
Net Pay	**$ 713.40**

Now let's say I sign up to have $100 taken out of each paycheck to go into my Flexible Spending Account for medical expenses. My paycheck will now look like this:

Weekly Gross Pay	**$ 1,000.00**
Federal Withholding	$ 134.52
Social Security	$ 55.80

Medicare	$ 13.05
State (6%)	$ 44.58
FSA	$ 100.00
Net Pay	**$ 652.05**

If you look carefully, you will see that I am paying $38.65 less in taxes. My net pay has only changed by $61.35 even though I am having $100 deducted. How does that work, you ask? Since the FSA contribution came out pre-tax, the $38.65 that WOULD have gone to taxes now comes to me as money I can use against medical expenses.

The Flexible Spending Accounts are helpful if you anticipate incurring any medical costs or childcare expenses over the course of the year. The only drawback is that if you do not have enough expenses to apply against whatever amount of money you have put into the account over the course of the year, you will forfeit the remaining balance. This rule comes from the IRS, not the company. But as you can see, FSA's can make your dollars go farther.

Employee & Dependent Life Insurance: This is always an odd discussion because you are considering a benefit that you will not ever gain anything from because...well...you will be dead. Nevertheless, even though you are relatively young, your death could result in expenses that your remaining assets will not be able to cover. Think about how much your family will need to cover whatever expenses you may leave behind.

I once had this conversation with a new campus hire and he was surprised at how much he would need to have in insurance if he wanted to leave this world with a balance of $0.00. The old adage is: "You cannot take it with you," but they failed to add "You can leave a big mess behind if you are not careful."

Before we continue, I need to define the type of life insurance you typically see from a company: it is called "term" insurance. As long as you pay the premiums, you have insurance. Stop paying the premiums, your insurance coverage stops. You have insurance for the period, or "term," that you pay the premiums. There are many different insurance products available on the market, but most companies offer term insurance because it is relatively cheap for employees and is easier to administer than other types of plans.

The new hire I mentioned had just graduated from a good business school and it was his first day on the job. As we reviewed his benefits, we came upon the topic of life insurance. He decided he was young and did not need any. Besides, if he died, his parents would get everything and they did not need the money. I asked him, will they get your debt, too? He thought about it and indicated that they just might. He asked about how much life insurance he could get and how much it would cost. I explained that since he was very young, the insurance would not be very much as our plans were term insurance and the rates were based upon age. The younger you are, the lower the rate.

As a matter of policy, our company provided employees with one times their annual salary in life insurance for free. Employees could then could buy up to five times their annual salary in additional life insurance if they so desired. I asked him how much he thought it would take to bring all of his debts to zero if he died right now. This is what we came up with:

Remaining student loans:	$ 28,000
Balance on credit cards:	$ 2,100
Balance on car loan:	$ 13,600
Expected funeral cost:	$ 6,000
Total Estimated Need:	**$ 49,700**

He came up with the idea to add in funeral costs, which I have to admit was a good idea. At that point, I started to feel like 'Bob the Insurance Guy' so I wanted to make sure I was not pushing him one way or the other. I just wanted him to make sure he understood his need, and I believe he did. Since his starting salary was $35,000, there was no way his company-provided life insurance of one times his salary was going to meet his needs, so he decided to go with two times his salary.

The other thing I will mention is that when you first enroll for benefits, you can usually sign up for the maximum amount of life insurance the company offers without having to prove you are actually in good health. If the employee in the above example wanted to raise the amount of life insurance he had to five times his salary at some future time, he would likely have to undergo health questions or evaluations to qualify. In other words, he would have to show proof of good health. Usually it is just a lengthy questionnaire written in Swahili, but at times it can involve being poked and prodded with sticks by disgruntled health-care workers.

Companies put this limitation out there because more often than not, someone will want to raise their life insurance because something is wrong with them, and they fear they may die sooner than expected. If you have any type of medical concerns that you think may limit your ability to get life insurance in the future, you may want to consider getting as much life insurance as you can afford through the company when you first enroll for benefits.

This raises another issue, and that is the insurance premiums companies charge for term life. They are not high rates, but in many cases, you may be able to get the same amount of life insurance coverage for less outside of the company. This is one benefit that you could save some money on by shopping for quotes from insurance agents or on the internet for comparison purposes.

Long-Term Disability Insurance (LTD): Long-Term Disability Insurance (also known as LTD) is an insurance that will provide you with replacement income if you become unable to perform the job for which you were trained. For example, if I worked on a production line that required me to stand for several hours at a time and developed a permanent medical condition that did not allow me to stand for more than an hour at a time, I could qualify for LTD. I can no longer do my job. In order for you to receive LTD payments, a condition typically has to be present for at least six months and there cannot be any other income source available to you. It typically provides you with 60% of the income you were receiving before your condition began. The rates you pay for this insurance are not very high, and where medical insurance protects you from unexpected high medical costs, LTD insurance provides you with a source of income if you are unable to work. This should not be confused with Sick Pay.

Sick Pay: Sick pay is a bank of time the company provides you to use in case you have a short-term illness like a cold or the flu. You usually begin with just a week or two of sick time to use in your first year, but as your time with the company increases, your bank of sick time may grow larger and larger. I can only surmise that this practice occurs because someone thought that the longer you are with a company, and the older you are, the more likely you are to get sick. Lovely.

Vacation: Like sick pay, vacation-time is a bank of time you can use when you need an excused absence from work. Unlike college, you do not get a week off from work in the fall, three weeks off over the holidays, a week off in the spring, and three months off in the summer. Nope, you are going to work year 'round. So if you want to take a trip to the beach or the mountains, you will need to make sure you have enough vacation-time to be out of the office AND your supervisor has approved you being out of the office and away from work.

HUH? I have to ask permission? Yes, unfortunately so. The good news is that you can go to the bathroom whenever you need to without permission or needing a hall pass, and there is no limit on the amount of visits you can make. But being away from the office does require permission because the people who will be counting on you need to know when you will be gone. Bummer.

In the mid 1990s, strange debilitating illnesses began creeping into workplaces that made employees feel like they had to use sick pay for "mental health days" in order to recover. Oddly enough, they would return the very next day refreshed, invigorated and sometimes even tan. After several years of in-depth management sessions and thousands of dollars spent on consultants, some companies determined that employees MAY be using their sick time as vacation. As a result, these same companies eliminated sick pay and vacation pay and replaced it with something called "Paid Time Off" (PTO) banks. These PTO banks provide employees with a few weeks a year of time that can be used as either vacation or sick time. Once this bank is used up, that's it. Shortly after the implementation of these PTO banks, outbreaks of the disease that required employees to take "mental health days" suddenly stopped. Ah, the miracles of modern medicine.

401K Plan: If you are 22-23 years old, you have approximately 42-43 years before you will be eligible for full retirement. Thoughts of retirement are somewhere on your "worry list," I'm sure...probably somewhere between the end of the world and the effects of a high cholesterol diet. I can't say that I blame you. It is somewhat hard to worry about something that will not happen until you have lived the equivalent of twice your current age. But there are significant financial benefits to thinking about this topic now, especially if your company offers a 401K plan with matching contributions. I will explain, and you can decide for yourself whether this is for you.

401K savings plans acquired their name from the portion of the Internal Revenue Service tax code that permits 401Ks to exist. If you are not familiar with the IRS, you will be as you get older. They are the folks who make sure you pay your fair share in taxes to the government so we can help the less fortunate, permit government services to operate, and generally keep America going. 401K plans permit you to have a certain amount of money deducted from your paycheck PRE-TAX (we've already discussed the benefits of pre-tax deductions) or post-tax, if you so desire, and to invest for the future. Most companies also match employee contributions going into your 401K plans, so you receive an extra bump to your savings. For example, if you contribute 6% of your pay to your 401K, your company may add an additional 3% of your pay to your account as a match. Not bad. Added up over time, this can create quite a nest egg that you can draw on when you are older to fund whatever you want to fund – vacations, bills, etc. Of course, there are limitations to the plan.

If you leave your company for another job and have not been there long enough to have a right to take the company contributions with you (we call this being "vested" in your company match) you would have to leave some or all of the employer money behind. Plus, just because you have left the company, it does not mean you can dip into the funds without penalty. Nope, the IRS rules limit you getting your hands on that money until you are 59 ½ years old, and any time it touches your hands before that age, you are going to pay taxes and penalties. Do some people spend the money, anyway? Yes, but you wonder how they'll feel years down the road when they have little to no money to retire on and have to work full-time until the day they die. Scary? Yes; but with proper planning, retirement will be a lot easier...and enjoyable.

Pension Plan: Your employer may or may not offer a pension plan for reasons I will explain below, but if they do, you need to understand what a pension plan offers. Under these plans, you will receive a monthly benefit at retirement that is derived from a formula based on your years of service with the company and your average salary over the last few years of your employment. The longer you are at the company, the bigger your monthly benefit will be. The first 10-15 years of your career, the calculated benefit is fairly low, but once someone hits about 20 years of company service and 50 years of age, the benefit begins to climb exponentially. The price for employees is very good, too; it is FREE. Yep, free. You do not pay anything for this benefit. You just show up everyday and do your job...for many years.

Pension plans used to be standard offerings at most companies, but they are not as prevalent as they used to be. Companies used to want employees to stay with them their entire career. But in the past ten years or so, the trend has been that employees work a few years at a company then move on, either on their own terms, or they are "downsized" and forced to move on. Mainly for these reasons, but also because these plans are very expensive to administer, many companies decided to do away with pensions and just go with 401Ks as their retirement savings benefit. But if your company does offer a pension plan, the one fact you need to know is that you will not be "vested" in any type of pension benefit until you have worked for the company for a certain length of time, usually five years. If you leave the company before that five year requirement is met, you will not be eligible for any benefit. Otherwise, there is not much you need to do with this benefit other than to know it exists.

Benefits can be complex to understand, especially if this is your first experience with them. But they are a sizable chunk of your total compensation, which is defined as the sum of your salary, plus any bonus you receive, plus the cost of the benefits the company pays on your behalf. Benefits are a good way to save some money for retirement and on certain expenses you may incur as a working professional. In the next chapter, one area we will talk about is how ignoring your "total compensation" can be a problem if you decide to leave your job and go work for someone else. Though there are more factors to consider when looking at a potential job change, "total compensation" is one element that needs to be included in your overall analysis. So, let's move on.

3.8 *Making a Change*

U p to this point in the book, we've talked about simply surviving your first year of your first real job. Completing your first year in one piece is a big event, so do take the time to stop and give yourself a standing ovation whenever you near the end of Year One. You may want to do this in private or after hours, but hey, we are celebrating, so whatever floats your boat. By the end of your first year, you will have seen and experienced many different things. You will be able to look back at where you were on Day One and see that you have indeed accumulated some knowledge that you did not have before you started your job. If you kept a journal of your first year, you will not only see your progress but be reminded of some things you had forgotten about. You will see that most of your first year is spent climbing a very steep learning curve and you really have very little time to think. Just about everything you do is a new experience and thus you are spending more time LEARNING about things than really DOING anything...or it may seem that way, at least.

Even though you have done a tremendous job surviving your first year, you may decide that wherever you are or whatever you are doing is just not your deal, and you want to make a change. You may think you are in the right job but in the wrong company culture. Or in the right company culture, but you just hate what you do. Or you may just dislike everything and everyone and figure you can't do much worse throwing a dart at the help wanted section of your local paper. Obviously, you are keen enough to know when you are not doing your best or not getting what you had hoped out of a particular situation. I am not going to venture into such topics as "How to Find Your High Paying/ Low Stress Dream Job Without Owning the Company" or "Interviewing Skills for the Unemployed Recluse" because there are hundreds of well-written/well-intentioned books on these topics already out there. Instead, I simply want to point out a few things to consider as you contemplate making a change.

Ask yourself "Is this situation really not working or am I just having a bout of frustration?" It is completely normal to find yourself frustrated with your job from time-to-time during your first year of working full-time. Don't forget you are still going through a change from student to full-time professional, whatever you may be doing. From structured to unstructured. From absolute answers to probable answers. Whenever you feel frustrated, wondering whether you are in the right line of work, right company, or right location, ask yourself, "Why exactly am I frustrated and was I this frustrated last week?" It could be that you are tired, hungry, sick, annoyed by family, annoyed by friends, angry over unexpected bills, etc. Any number of things could be piled up in your subconscious basket and this last little work crisis/event/problem could just have pushed you over the edge.

If you get to the point that all your introspection and research tells you that this job just is not working out and you need to make a change, give serious thought to what you are looking to find. Your current job is lacking something you need. What is it?

Look at your current job in each of the following areas for possible clues:

Your boss: Most employees leave their jobs because of their boss, so this is the first area to consider. Maybe your boss is a poor manager (no direction, no communication), something about his/her personality does not mesh well with yours, or maybe devotion to the job is a top priority for your boss and you want more out of life than 24/7 in the office.

To discover what may be going on in your relationship with your boss, ask yourself the two questions below:

- In what ways do my boss and I work well, and
- What would I change about the way my boss and I interact, if I could?

Write a brief paragraph (at least) answering each of these questions on a sheet of paper, or a journal if you are keeping one, then move on to the next section.

Where you work: As we've discussed, company cultures vary dramatically from one to the other. It could be that you do not feel comfortable in your current company's culture. Maybe you are laid back and feel smothered by the high degree of formality and conservative ideals. Or, maybe you prefer a more structured, orderly environment and not one where every day seems to be completely different from the next. To determine what may be happening between you and the company you work for, ask yourself these three questions:

- What attracted me to this company to begin with?
- What have I liked about working here?
- What have I found to be different from what I expected?

As with the previous section, record your answers and move on to the final section.

What you do: Work is probably not the first thing on your list when it comes to how you would choose to spend your free time. We have to work to make a living, though, so most of us try to find something in the job that gives us a degree of pleasure and satisfaction so we can continue to do it day after day. After your first year, you may not be feeling as challenged as you expected to be. School may have prepared you for the more analytical, complex type of work that you have yet to experience in your day-to-day job. For the first year of your first job, that is to be expected. Most of what you may end up doing during your first year may not require much of the knowledge you received in school.

This will change as years go by. The more experience you gain in a particular line of work, the more likely you are to receive projects and encounter situations that require you to utilize all the training and education you gained in school. Bosses can change, but there is no guarantee your next one will be any better than the first. Company cultures rarely change without some catastrophic, titanic failure (i.e., Enron). But work can morph over time from mundane and routine, to complex and unpredictable. It just takes a little time for that type of work to appear for a first year employee.

But if your situation is markedly different from what I just described, maybe you should consider another position with another employer. This is never an easy call, though, and even upon further review, changing jobs may or may not be the right answer. To determine what may be happening between you and the work you do, ask yourself these questions:

- What types of things do I enjoy doing in my free time?
- Does my job offer any opportunity to experience some of the things I enjoy doing in my free time? For example, if you love to be outdoors but work in an office building, this could be a negative connection between what you like and what your job offers. But if you like to read in your spare time and you work as a paralegal (who has to read a lot), that may be a positive connection.
- When I was in school training for _____, I envisioned my work

days would be filled with what type of activities?

- Now that I am working, what have I found to be different from what I expected?

As with the previous sections, record your answers and now look at this collection of information in its entirety. The intent of this exercise is to force you to articulate what you like and do not like in a boss, in a company's culture and/or in the content of whatever work you do. You have basically completed a self-interview about all the aspects of your current situation. You now have expert information about what may be going on with you in your current job.

Why is this important? Once you have a better idea about how your preferences run in each of these areas, you can get an idea of what is not working in your current job and what you should look for in a new opportunity. As you look at other opportunities, you need to compare them to the list you just developed. Are those characteristics there? Are the things you DO NOT like there? Have an idea about what you want in a new position and stay focused on that. If your "ideal situation" changes along the way, that is fine, but whatever happens, you should maintain your focus on where you want to go instead of where you have come from.

In addition, as I mentioned in the previous chapter, you need to consider your "total compensation" and how that could be impacted by any job change. When folks start to think about changing jobs, their first inclination is to look at their current salary versus the salary they are offered with the new position. That is valid because your salary pays your bills, helps you save for retirement, etc. However, you also need to include the value of your benefits package in your comparison. Benefits, more or less, run about 34% of your salary. For example, if you make $50,000, the company is likely contributing another $17,000 towards the cost of your benefits. That is a hunk of change if you had to come up with it out of your own pocket. You may not see this money in "cash," but you do see it in the form of lower insurance premiums and costs associated with providing the plans.

I mention this because I had a co-worker who grumbled about his pay at least once a week. One day he came in and announced he was resigning because he had a great offer from another company. It was a great offer salary-wise and according to him, it had an unbelievable bonus package. Who could blame him for taking it? We had a big going away lunch, wished him well, and he was gone. Months later, I heard through a friend that he had left that job and had come back to our company in a lower position than what he had left. Why? Because the company he went to offered such poor benefits he was actually losing money. His new company offered no retirement plans, very limited medical insurance that had high premiums and high deductibles (which means he had to pay more cash out of his pocket to cover medical expenses), and a bonus plan that rarely paid out. So, you have to look at both pay AND benefits when you look at your total compensation, otherwise you may be leaving money on the table.

The danger you are trying to avoid is running FROM your current job. You will definitely be able to find another job out there in the big wide world, but if you simply accept another job to get away from your gosh-awful mess of a position at blah, blah, blah company, you could fall into a worse situation than what you were in before. Instead, you want to run TO a better opportunity, one that you are genuinely charged up about because you know what you like and do not like. At least on the surface, this new opportunity should offer the characteristics you like. Running TO an opportunity limits the chance that you could be out job shopping again in a year or so.

Too often I see resumes of people who worked at a location for a year, then moved to another job at another company, usually in the same role. In year three it was apparently time to move again, so off they went, only to land somewhere else eighteen months later. After seeing a second move in such a short time, I could only think that this person either cannot hold a job or does not know what they want. Either way, they are not someone I am interested in speaking with for a potential opportunity because I do not perceive they would stay around very long.

No matter if your first year in your first job is fantastic or just so-so, one thing you should plan to do on a regular basis is update your resume. A resume is a record of what you have accomplished over the course of your career, a history of your professional life much like your college transcript was a history of your college coursework. If you keep your resume up-to-date, you will have the best possible record of the experience you have gained whenever you need it. Otherwise, you will be tasked with trying to pull together this history from memory at some point in the future. Since our memories are not always complete and accurate, you run the risk of leaving important details out of your personal history when you do not update your resume on a regular basis.

For example, if I asked you to tell me from memory what you were doing on the third Tuesday of June five years ago in explicit detail, could you do it? Probably not. Our memories tend to lose the detail around specific activities as time goes by. These recollections of past events become more generalized as time passes with only the occasional surprise of a specific fact popping out of some crevice way back in our brain. I bet you can recall the perfume or cologne your first car date was wearing the night you went out. I bet you even remember the movie you saw and the dinner you ate. That is a special occasion, one of those "in the crack of my brain" memories that is easier to pull out and think about than most.

But now tell me what movie you went to on your *third* date with that person. Difficult? Perplexing? Impossible? That is because this detail is likely gone for good. In much the same manner, little details about skills and job experiences you had can slip away if you do not make a conscious effort to maintain the "history of you." It will be much easier on you if you begin reviewing your resume once a month, or once a quarter, to see if you have had a professional gain worth noting and adding to your resume. You likely will put significant energy and time into any new professional experience or expertise that you gain over the course of your career journey. Do not let it be forgotten.

Considering a job change is never easy and especially one so early in your career. You likely started your current job with a lot of hopes and expectations that have not come to pass, and the disappointment can be heavy. It may feel that you have failed, but do not let yourself believe that. You have not failed. We all must remember that our professional lives are just a small piece of who we are, and you are no exception. Realizing our full potential as human beings requires not only our energy and dedication to making difficult situations work but also our honesty to acknowledge when situations are not working.

In the same spirit that we embrace a strategic retreat when we are trying to carry forward an issue that cannot give us a meaningful victory, we must embrace the same belief when we are faced with continuing an endeavor that will bring us no gain. Acknowledge that you are not in a positive situation and be willing to make a change…for you are only making your future better.

Section 4 – Maintain Perspective

LEAVING CAMPUS

LEAVING CAMPUS

4.1 The Roles You Play

When I was growing up I had a large sugar maple outside of my bedroom window. To a young boy, each tree offers the potential to be a natural jungle gym, a lookout post, or a threat to wooden gliders launched from a bedroom window. Each Fall the limbs on this sugar maple would explode in a rolling exhibition of color as the leaves turned from bright yellow through orange to fluorescent red-orange before finally dying away for the season and forming an easy supply of natural confetti for us kids to use in many creative ways.

Our neighbors would stop by our house on their walks and comment on how beautiful the leaves were, especially against the deep blue sky that accompanies a Tennessee autumn, and how of all the trees around our house, that was one they just could not miss. For the rest of the year, however, no one, except for me, paid much attention to the tree. No one stopped on their walks to comment on how cool the shade must be under its dense foliage on a July day, or how in the Spring, the broad branches provided such secure, solid shelter to the nest of robins that made their home there each year. Or how if you really knew what you were doing in the Winter, you could drill a hole in the sunny side of the tree, tap in a small tube, hang a bucket and have the makings of real honest to goodness maple syrup. My sugar maple had many other roles than just producing beautiful leaves in the Fall, but no one seemed to notice. No one noticed but me.

I use this illustration to point out that like my sugar maple, you, too, have other roles than just your work role, even though that is where we have spent most of our time.

Your 'work role' may be the one that gets the most attention or consumes the most time in your life right now, but that is only a part of the person you are. Lately you may not have had time to think about the other pieces of you and how they are doing, since your first year can consume most of your physical, emotional and mental energy.

But I believe you have three distinct roles in your life, whether you know it or not. It is an individual call for each person about which role will/can/should take precedence in their life, or whether all roles will be treated with equal respect. More difficult still is how to manage each of those roles without detriment to one of the others. As this is still early in your adult life, you may not have a clue regarding what I am talking about, so let me walk you through what I perceive to be our three roles in life.

The three roles I see us all having are:

1. The "Me" Role
2. The "We" Role
3. The "Us" Role

Let's discuss each in a little more detail.

The "Me" Role. The "Me" Role is the role in which you focus on taking care of your personal needs. As we discussed earlier, you are on your own and no one else is going to take care of you. It is all your ballgame now. What type of needs are you responsible for? You are responsible for the obvious things like finding a safe place to live, having food to eat, and paying your bills to keep the lights on. Also, you are now accountable for meeting the needs you have as a functioning human being. There are many aspects to the "Me" Role, but all relate to your role in taking care of yourself. Let's discuss health as an example.

You are still at an age where you can consume an entire super-jumbo cheeseburger meal (with a regular soda) every night for a week, lay on the couch for several hours until its time for bed, and not gain a pound. Exercise, you say? Why? I do not see the point? Yeah, I know you don't. But I am sad to say that your hyper-bionic metabolism will not continue forever. One day you will find that, instead of the scenario I described above, you will eat amazingly bland food, exercise every night for a week between the time you get home and the time you go to bed, and still not LOSE a pound!

Starting up an active lifestyle now (or maintaining one you may already have) is a good way to make sure that you are getting exercise for your health and for burning enough calories to keep your weight manageable. Your diet will play a big part in this, as well. Yes, there will be nights where after a long day you just do not feel like preparing anything for dinner, and those bright yellow fast food signs look oh so appealing. But whenever possible, you need to make sure you are getting a balanced, healthy diet of the appropriate food groups as recommended by the Food and Drug Administration (you are paying taxes now, you may as well get some benefit from the government).

Proper diet and exercise is also a way to reduce any stress that you get from your work or other endeavors. By eating properly and keeping your body active, you not only get short term benefits like stress reduction and weight management, you also make an investment in your future by lowering your risk of conditions like high blood pressure and stroke, just to name two.

One need I found hardest to adjust to when I first started working was the need for sleep. I was so used to school providing me with automatic time off for spring break, fall break, summer break, etc., that I had never had to monitor my schedule to make sure I was getting the sleep my body needed. I could burn myself out during the semester but when break time came, I could recharge my battery by doing absolutely nothing, and I would be ready to roll again the next semester. The first year of my first job, though, I did not get that semester break. Seeing the summer come and go knowing I would not have a big break coming up was quite difficult. A full-time job, I learned, goes twelve months a year with only the two weeks of vacation, and occasional holidays, to break the monotony. Yuck.

Not only was my first year crammed full of work days, but my work days were crammed full, too! I had heard tales of forty hour work weeks before I started working but in reality, they were more like fifty-plus hour weeks if I did not work efficiently. In fact, between a longer commute to get to work, a busier day, and the new obligations related to my own care and feeding, I had to start getting up much earlier than I ever had before just to stay on top of things. This was a big switch from my 'sleep until eight o clock, grab a fast breakfast, hit class for a few hours, and then lounge around for the rest of the day' life of college.

In my old life, I could stay up all hours of the night and still be fine the next day because I could sleep a little later and hopefully get rested up (assuming a few naps on the couch, of course). Not with a full-time job. Since I HAD to be at work the next day, the quality of rest I received the night before directly correlated with how together I was the next day. If I had a good night's sleep the night before, I felt clear-headed, on top of things, and reasonably aware of what I had to do at work. If I was out late with friends or neglected to get the amount of sleep my body needed, I felt it. I was tired, unfocused and my thought process did not flow like it should. Even my hearing seemed to be amiss. Someone would come into my office and say:

"I saw John in the hall today and he indicated a concern about his upcoming leave of absence. I told him he could talk to you about it but I wanted to make sure I understood how everything worked with our leave practices first. I did not say much to John but realized I am about as informed as he is. Can you help me understand how leaves of absence work?"

What I HEARD in my exhausted state was more akin to:

"Any skyscraper can conquer a tuba player, and it takes a real diskette to find subtle faults with the most difficult umbrella. The paper napkin can try to seduce a bullfrog, but the South American cowboy is the only one who can give a pink slip to a cheese wheel from an avocado pit."

Ok, so maybe that is not really what I heard, but it may not be far off. One of the areas directly affected by a lack of sleep is my listening comprehension. I really have to pay close attention to what someone is saying to me when I am exhausted. Otherwise, I cannot seem to put the pieces together. Adequate rest is critical to my ability to function.

Spiritual needs are also a part of this role. These are very personal needs, and depending on the person, the need can be very high or very low. How you address any spiritual, or faith, needs is a highly individual decision. You may have grown up active in a religious institution and had your spiritual need met on a very steady basis in your younger years. But even though you are older now and may be in another town, city, or state, your need may still exist. This is a need that is not easily ignored or replaced by some other activity; therefore part of your "Me" Role may be to seek out a place where you can continue to grow spiritually. Or, you may have been raised without any spiritual influence in your life, but now that you are out on your own, you may discover an emptiness you never had before. Could this be a need for spiritual growth or a need to understand your role in the greater picture of the world and eternity? It may not be clear, but again, like every other aspect of this role, it is an area that will be up to you to meet.

Another aspect of this role can be your need for intellectual stimulation and growth. Though your job may be challenging and stimulating, it only develops a portion of your intellectual capability. You may even find that you will grow more curious about topics you hated when you were in school. I know when I began to work I developed interests in Egyptian history and photography. Yes, I knew where Egypt was when I was in school ("Somewhere over there" is how I would put it) and I liked clicking pictures with my simple camera when on vacation with family or just in the mood to do something different. But my interest was limited to what I needed to know to either pass a test or take a picture.

After starting work, however, I found myself wanting to know more about the history of Egypt and the progress that civilization had made such a long time ago. With photography, I developed an interest in the many different ways you could manipulate a camera to get a desired picture. The pictures throughout this book are the result of that interest. If you have ever studied photography, you know there are many complex aspects that go into good photography. It may still be too early for you to be developing interests in new areas, but chances are it will happen as your need for intellectual stimulation increases.

There are many other aspects to the "Me" Role, but hopefully you received a sense of the areas I am including in this role. Your body, soul and mind all have needs which must be met in order to help you be a functional human being. In the same way poor car maintenance leads to the eventual failure of the car, neglecting your "Me" Role can cause your person to experience failures of its own. Though the needs vary from person-to-person, the common factor among all of us is that our personal needs must be addressed in some way. The "Me" Role carries that responsibility.

The "We" Role. In your "We" Role, you are responsible for meeting and maintaining the needs associated with your work life and professional acquaintances. All jobs vary drastically from person to person. It is difficult to pin down specifics related to this role, but it basically is related to all the time, energy and effort you spend towards doing whatever you do for a living. I called this the "We" Role because all jobs require someone else to get things done. Even a small business person who has no employees needs to partner with the customers to be successful.

I also refer to this role as the "Replaceable Role" for a very specific reason: in your job, like it or not, you are replaceable. Yes, we will miss your smile and your snappy comebacks, but if you leave, another person will fill your seat doing pretty much the same thing you were doing in much the same way. For the majority of us who work for a living, there will always be someone out there who can slide into our role and do it equally well, and sometimes better, than we do. This is true for any one of us, from the CEO on down. CEO's retire, die, go to prison, etc., but even with those roles, a new person slides into the job, and with a hefty bonus and a hearty share of stock options, they help the company continue on. My job will never have the scale and scope of a CEO, so why do I think my replacement value would be any different? It is not. It is a replaceable role.

The "Us" Role. The "Us" Role deals with meeting and maintaining the needs associated with your personal relationships. In this role, you simply cannot be replaced. You are replaceable at work and in your professional relationships but in this role, you are irreplaceable. Only you can be the child that you are to your parents, or your spouse's husband or wife. Only you can provide these people with the unique presence that is you and you alone.

I call this role the "Us" Role as "Us" implies a level of intimacy that "We" Roles just do not hold. The "Us" Role allows us to like, care for and love who the person is and to know what they are all about. "We" Roles rarely move closer than just a handshake and a hearty smile. In "We" Roles we know faces, but in our "Us" Roles, we know hearts.

Each of these roles has its own place in our lives. In a perfect situation, we would have all the time necessary to devote to each role to ensure a completely satisfying and fulfilling experience for ourselves and those around us. But it is not a perfect world. Our life is measured in limited pockets of time, each with varying starting points, lengths, and end points. Whether we are talking about our age (i.e., twenty-five years old), a life phase (the teenage years), or a specific period of the year (i.e., the Holiday Season), these are specific measurement phrases that when we hear them, we know exactly how much time the phrase is indicating. What this implies, however, is that time is finite and we only have a set amount of time in which to live our lives. Though there is much in our world we can control and change if we do not like what we are dealt, we are without choice when it comes to the constraint time places upon our lives. There is no choice but to submit to it.

One underlying fact you must remember is that the amount of time you have to address each of your three roles never gets any greater. You only have twenty-four hours in each day, seven days in each week, and three hundred sixty five days in each year, to live your life. You cannot create more time to accommodate your roles. Since you are allocating a fixed amount over several choices, some area has to give up time in order for another area to gain that same time.

Thus the conundrum. Here you stand with three roles to play, each distinct and difficult in their own right, much less as a combined trio. Overriding these roles is the constraint of Time, out of our control and unyielding in its limits. These all must come together in a way that is most effective for you. You are left with a simple decision: how will you allocate the time you have to the roles you fill? Equal shares of time to all? If not, which role gains? Which one loses? Do we know the cost of each decision and are we O.K. with the price?

For most of your first year you may have been able to keep yourself fairly balanced among your life roles. You may have gone to work and still had time to spend with significant people in your life as well as keep yourself well fed, exercised and rested. After all, it IS your first year and expectations and responsibilities are still relatively light. What I want you to keep in mind, however, is that over time, ever so slowly, your roles can unknowingly become disproportionate. This disproportionate allocation can sneak up on you, little by little, without your knowledge until it simply becomes a way of life...a way of life that you may not have intended but are now contending with, desired or not. How does this happen?

Becoming unbalanced can happen by taking on a little more responsibility here and there over the course of time. You do not notice the increase because it is so subtle and slight until you one day look back and think, wow, how did I get so busy? What happened? It can happen with any aspect of your life in any of the roles; it is not limited to happening in just one area. It happens in the "We" Role because you take on more and more responsibility in your professional career as you gain more experience. It happens in the "Me" Role when personal needs and fixations slowly grow from habits to compulsions. It can happen in "Us" relationships when they grow from being healthy relationships to co-dependent ones where you become consumed by either each other or some negative behavior like alcohol or drug addiction that you share.

If you are at least aware of becoming unbalanced, you can hopefully avoid becoming a victim of what I call "role creep." "Role creep" is when you slowly become unbalanced as one or more of your roles begin to rule your life before you know it. I believe avoiding "role creep" is particularly important at this stage of your career because you are building your habits for the future and are flexible enough to modify habits as needed.

You may want to focus more on one role than another, and if so, that is your call. You just need to understand and plan for how this focus will affect your other roles going forward. If you want balance across your roles, that is your call, as well. Again, you just need to understand what this would look like and be willing to accept the pain and pleasure that comes with these decisions.

Following are general narratives outlining some general pros and cons to each role choice for you to read and consider. My purpose with presenting information in this manner is not to be a complete resource on the pros and cons of these decisions, but to illustrate how there are consequences to each choice you could make…both positive and negative. There are no right answers to questions like these — only the end result that reflects the choices you make. But in order to start considering your choices, you first must be aware of what they are.

"Me" Focused Scenario. In the "Me" Focused scenario, you may find that overall you gain exceptional wellness in the physical, spiritual and psychological areas of your life. If your self-image is driven or enhanced by your physical condition, you may have a higher than average self-image due to the commitment you have made to the "Me" Role. If your "Me" commitment has included attending to your spiritual needs, you may find you are more confident and secure in the broader aspects of your life, as well.

On the flip side, however, you run the risk of being severely impacted by mental or emotional aspects of a physical injury or illness. Such a situation would limit your ability to keep yourself in optimal physical and/or spiritual shape. As a large degree of your self-confidence or self-image may be derived from your physical condition or appearance, you may feel the emotional pain equally severally as the physical discomfort.

From a career perspective, are you comfortable with your job simply being a source of income? Like it or not, a certain degree of dedication to your job is required to at least be viewed as a solid contributor. Will your focus on the "Me" Role allow you enough time and energy to commit to delivering a solid performance for whoever employs you? Without this commitment, you may find that it is difficult to keep your job, much less grow professionally, in order to better your standard of living.

I am not talking about devoting all your waking hours to your job. Instead, I am simply talking about giving 100% effort to your work while you are at work instead of being distracted by thoughts of other things you could be doing to grow your "Me" Role. If you are ok with just having a job to provide a source of income to enable the growth of your "Me" Role, then that is fine. But if you also expect that you will see increasing rewards from your job while maintaining an overweight focus on your "Me" Role, these two expectations may be in conflict.

What about your relationships with other people? One risk of a "Me" Focused role is it may be difficult to grow meaningful relationships with others. Since a "Me" Focused role requires you to look out for your best interests and welfare, this focus may limit your ability to put yourself aside when necessary to grow closer to others. This is especially true in romantic type relationships when it takes the dedicated effort of both parties to make love work. You may think you are willing to devote the time and energy to the personal relationships in your life. But when faced with having to choose between your "Me" Role and the "Us" Role obligations, you may find yourself overly protective of your "Me" Role simply because that is where you have focused so much of your energy for most of the time.

"We" Focused Scenario. In the "We" Focused scenario, significant focus is placed on your career and professional relationships. Because of the high level of attentiveness placed on these relationships, you may experience a faster than normal career progression in your field. Though relationships are part of the "We" Focused role, the biggest commitment you will make with this focus is your time. You may feel extremely satisfied with your career because the time you commit allows you to stay on top of things. You are willingly where you need to be whenever you need to be there in order to focus on this role. If you have a high need to achieve and succeed, this need should be met by your fast moving career. You may start to see a higher than normal amount of financial rewards coming your way, which can lead to a feeling of financial security and stability in your life.

On the flip side, you run the risk of experiencing disenchantment with your career or even a touch of depression if you do not feel the results of your time commitment meet your aspirations. In other words, if your career does not go as far or as fast as you want it to (which is why you committed all the time to it in the first place), you could get discouraged. Because the "We" Role takes such a large amount of your attention, you may find that outside of the responsibilities of your "We" Role, you do not have many other areas of interest in your life.

Because of the limited amount of time available outside of the "We" Role, you may find your physical, emotional and spiritual needs go unmet or are lacking. Lack of sleep and poor diet can result in persistent fatigue. Failure to exercise can result in higher than normal levels of stress. If there are medical conditions that are adversely affected by a lack of exercise and poor diet (i.e., high blood pressure), the symptoms from those conditions may be compounded. You may experience frustration if any part of your self-confidence is driven by your self image and your self-image is impacted as described above.

Your "Us" Roles may also suffer because of your "We" Role focus. Because "We" Roles are job related, and your job usually requires your presence somewhere else (i.e., work) in order to make your contribution to the role, you simply may not have enough time to be with other individuals to either initiate or grow lasting "Us" Roles. You are always at the office, the hospital, traveling on assignment, or some other location away from those who value your "Us" Role. The "Us" Roles you do maintain may be more similar to your business or professional contacts than to true, intimate "Us" Roles. The longer "Us" Roles are neglected, the less connection is there. Since your "We" focus already limits the time you have to grow your intimate "Us" relationships, it is not likely you will be able to find the time to repair any damage that may have occurred to your "Us" Roles.

"Us" Focused Scenario. In the "Us" Focused scenario, you may find that focusing on this area provides you with richer personal relationships, either in the form of a few deep relationships or many acquaintances spread across a wide spectrum of personality types. Filling your "Us" Role requires a strong dedication of your emotional energy because personal relationships grow from the sharing of intimate thoughts, feelings and dreams with others. If you have a strong need for and gain strength from the interaction with people on a personal level, this need should be met with the "Us" Focused role. You may gain a great deal of emotional satisfaction from the relationships this focus nurtures.

On the flip side, breakdowns within the "Us" Focused role can create a high level of emotional anxiety. In the same manner that the "Us" Focused role provides a great deal of emotional satisfaction when the relationships developed by this focus are going well, an equally high level of emotional dissatisfaction can result when the relationships do not go well. Because you have put so much of yourself into these roles on a personal level, it is easier to be hurt by breakdowns in these relationships than relationships of a more casual nature. Emotional pain is much more difficult to simply dismiss. If you know someone casually through school or work and have a disagreement, it may bother you for a bit, but you will likely get over it in a day or so. With "Us" relationships, a disagreement (or worse) with one in whom you have placed all your trust, hopes and dreams is not as easy to get over…if you ever get over it at all. Because the "Us" Role has been your main focus and likely a steady, solid anchor in your life, you may feel adrift if the relationship goes away. This feeling of instability may continue indefinitely until another relationship evolves that allows you to become "Us" Focused again.

The "Me" Role can be either helped or hurt by an "Us" focus. For example, if your "Us" relationships are ones that value the benefits of healthy lifestyles, intellectual bantering, or spiritual growth, you may actually see your "Me" Role grow, as well. But if the group dynamics support potentially damaging behaviors such as binge drinking, discourage pursuits that grow your intellectual capabilities, or ridicule any attempts at spiritual growth, your "Me" Role may be adversely affected.

From a "We" Role standpoint, any high level career aspirations are not likely to be fully met due to the time committed to the "Us" Role. Your career may be solid, but not exceptional, and may be more of a "means to an end." This implies that your job would be solely a source of income that permits you to do other things that give you greater satisfaction and pleasure outside of work. This may be absolutely fine with you. You just need to be comfortable with your current job or role because you may not move any higher than where you are right now.

"Balanced" Focused Scenario. In the Balanced Focused scenario, you attempt, as much as possible, to allocate your time equally across all your roles. Whether you have met this goal is not measured on a daily basis but across a broader period: a month, six months, or a year. You may be focused on one role for a week or two and thus for the short term, you can appear unbalanced. Over the course of a greater period, however, you should appear more balanced across the roles. The Balanced Focus may provide you with a richer, more diverse life due to the diversity of the roles. Each role gets attention from you and in return, you are enriched with what that role brings to your life. Overall, you may experience a feeling of peace or contentment from being on top of things, knowing each of your roles is being nourished.

On the flip side, the Balanced Focus may create frustration from time-to-time. Since your focus is broad (covering all roles) but not particularly deep in any one role, you may feel like you are not accomplishing anything significant in any one area. You may perceive yourself to be an average contributor to each role. You may also find frustration when attempting to monitor whether you are indeed balanced across the roles. It is difficult to measure, and sometimes you may have to rely on feedback from others, which is not always objective.

You may want to experiment with one of the above scenarios, trying each until you find a distribution that best fits your needs. You may choose to focus on one of your roles or you may choose to incorporate a balanced approach to the roles that you have. There are pros and cons with each scenario, but whether one scenario is better for you than another scenario will be a completely personal choice. We all have different needs, wants and desires and what may be the obvious choice for one may not be for another. But as long as you understand the concept of your three roles and how they can be affected by the limitation of Time, you have learned what I wanted you to know.

4.2 Balance

In this first year of your first real job, allocation of roles is just one of many decisions you will face as you take the reins of adulthood. Life from this point forward will unfortunately give you fewer and fewer decisions that carry an obviously right or obviously wrong answer for you. Instead, you will be faced with situations where one option may be relatively better or worse than other options you could take, but there likely will not be an absolute choice. How you allocate your life is one of those decisions.

We describe these types of decisions as having 'shades of gray,' meaning that you can see good points and bad points to each decision. These types of decisions are hard for people to make and some people need a lot of time to make these types of decisions. They need time to look at all the options, weigh out the pros and cons, and become comfortable with committing one way or another. Others don't need as much time because they will just review the situation, look at a few key factors, and choose one option over the other.

I am more like the first type of decision maker; the long, slow thinking type. A difficult decision faced me when I had to decide how to end this book. Why? Because this is how I will leave you. Someone once told me, "Always leave someone as if you will never see them again," meaning the last word you say to them or the last glance you give them may be how they remember you. Try to make that last memory a good one. That said, I almost ended this book on the topic of money because, honestly, that is a big reason why any of us work. If everything was free, we would spend our time pursuing opportunities which meet the particular needs and passions that lie in each of us. How wonderful that would be. But in reality, we need a certain amount of income to pay bills, buy food and provide shelter for ourselves and our families. As a result, we must sell our services to the highest bidder in return for monetary compensation to meet the financial needs in our life. But that is not what we are all about, at least not from where I sit. And that's not the thought I wanted to leave you with.

Instead, I chose to end this book on keeping your life in perspective and giving attention to the various roles you have. You are an individual whose talents and gifts stretch well beyond the confines of your career. Many years from now you may be doing something completely different professionally than what you trained for in college, or maybe you will still love what you went to school to be. I sincerely hope that what you choose to do for a living gives you a degree of satisfaction and enjoyment. Otherwise, it will be a long wait until retirement. As a friend once advised me, "You don't want to spend your time wishing your life away." But tied to this wish for your satisfaction with work and professional career is a simple caution about keeping it all in perspective.

I feel at this point that I need to share a bit of personal insight about me. I believe strongly in authors putting something of themselves on the table so you can get a sense of where they are coming from and why they feel the way they do. Therefore I am going to follow my belief and provide some insight into where I am at this point in my life.

This perspective is from one who traveled the same road you have just started down, only I began my journey fourteen years ago. For that reason, I will share my story thus far, in the hope you can glean a bit of insight for you to use as you travel the same highway.

This book has focused on building a solid foundation in your career during the first year of your first real job. Each morning (or evening if you work nights) when you rise to meet the day, I hope you will accept the responsibilities of your work role, give your best and meet your commitments, and continue to build your skills and qualifications in whatever profession you have chosen to enter. Regardless of what you do professionally, however, do not forget the other two facets of who you are – give those roles the same attention as you have just given your work role. Why?

If you do not keep yourself balanced, you run the risk of your job becoming the identity of who you are. As we discussed earlier, the more you put into your job life, the less there is for the other roles you have. Your "Me" and "Us" Roles will whither and fade and all you will have left is your professional career...your "We" Role. If your job, for whatever reason, would go away, then theoretically the person you are would go away. What will you have left if that happens?

When I was still relatively new to the working world, I became very close with a senior manager who had many years with the company and was approaching a point where it made more financial sense for him to retire than keep working. His pension service was maxed out, he was approaching the full retirement age, and he had more than enough resources to sustain a very comfortable lifestyle for the rest of his life. He would ask me various questions about his retirement options, and I would joke with him by saying that he had decisions to make that I could not wait to have – when to retire and start enjoying life!

During one of our conversations I mentioned that again, and he stopped and said, "You know, this job is all I have. If I retire, I don't know what I will do. This company has been everything I am. I have worked so much that I really do not have many friends outside of work, and my wife and I are not that close any more. I don't know how I will fill my days."

Driving home that evening, our conversation replayed itself over and over in my mind. I was both haunted by his comments and confused by his view, a frustrating combination to a young mind. As a relatively inexperienced employee, it was inconceivable to me that retirement, with all its opportunities, would not be attractive to someone. As years went by, however, I started to see the trap he had found himself in, the slow migration into an unbalanced life that is so easy to find yourself living.

I began to notice people who once had driving ambition begin to stagger under the weight of its demands. There was no joy or fire to their lives anymore, and for most, work was all they had. Years of working long hours and weekends, ignoring family and friends for meager increases to support a lifestyle beyond their means left them with no identity. Their jobs were it. As their jobs faded away from cost-cutting and layoffs, I would watch them also fade away with nothing to mark their passing but a dusty keyboard and a worn-out telephone. Gone…as if they were never there.

As years passed, I began to realize I was one of them. One of the corporate animals who was willing and ready to jump through that next little hoop, only to find that the size of the hoop kept changing…if there was even a hoop there at all. I started to feel disconnected and lost, seeing myself doing and producing things but feeling strangely empty. When I started working, I held the hope that as years went by, I would always see and appreciate the richness that life holds, both professionally and personally. But I was beginning to see I was not building that life. That was a sad realization for me…the person I wanted to be, and the person I was becoming, were not the same.

Before I began working, I had an appreciation for what I now define as 'simple moments.' My new work life, however, did not allow the time for such things as I had to always be "on," in business mode, to contemplate the next set of problems at the office. In retrospect, I think I sometimes created work dilemmas in my mind to worry over because it made me feel like I was accomplishing something while I was away from work…the place where my heart seemed to be. I was growing numb, and I did not like it. I struggled with this for many months before finally realizing why I had become so lost on my journey.

I was not valuing the complete person I was. I was pouring all that I had, both physically and emotionally, into my work and had no time for anything else. Since I was not actively participating in the growth of my personal life, I found myself searching in vain to find some small speck that I could point to in my career that would give me some type of personal fulfillment. Repeatedly, though, I failed. Yet, I would keep trying, trudging on while the special moments of life passed me by…too trivial to be given time. I tolerated each with a reserved impatience and for the first time in my life, I felt unhappy. Not depressed or stressed, just unhappy. Robert Louis Stevenson once said, "There is no duty we underrate so much as the duty of being happy." The truth of his wisdom was becoming crystal clear.

Questions about my life and my purpose began to flow, most with obviously simple answers, but answers I subconsciously ignored because they were not complex enough. In retrospect, my intelligence led to my stupidity as I viewed a life filled with complexity and chaos as successful. But I was wrong. I wonder sometimes what memories I missed during that portion of my life when I would not give much thought or time to anything but work and my career. I grieve in a way for that period of my life, even now, because I know that some moments have passed forever and I can never get them back. But at least I came to realize that my life was not going where I wanted it to go before it was too late, and that I had the power to change the way things were. I still had time to create the type of life that mattered to me, and for that realization, I am truly thankful.

Since that time, I have tried to take the balanced approach to life, although I will be the first to admit I slip up every once and awhile. It is not easy by any stretch in this day and age. Overall, though, the years since that time have been filled with wonderful experiences with wonderful people in wonderful places. Many of them were within my professional capacity, but an equal number fell within my own journey of increasing self-awareness about who I am and within those roles that only I fill – father, husband, and son.

As time goes by, I start to find that I am not alone in being more than just my work. Every now and then I stumble across a kindred spirit dedicated to a balanced life, struggling to keep the horizon level in a working world that seems to desire your very soul. None of us who aspire to the balanced life may change the world, but we may make a few more memories along the way than we would have otherwise. We can honestly say we give our best in our jobs, and even gain a bit of satisfaction from seeing the results of our labors. But our jobs only get a portion of who we are. I do not know how high my career may go or whether I will even be in my chosen profession in one, five, or ten years. But I have decided to have a life that requires my participation in multiple roles beyond just my "We" Role, and for that, I willingly sacrifice any claim to title and power.

I like to think that I and others like me may see a few more years added to our lives because we realized the "Me" values of health, spirit and mind before it was too late. The commitment made to a balanced life may also give us a few more opportunities to hold our children before they leave our arms forever for adulthood. When sadness touches our hearts, there will be arms to hold us as we cry because we made the effort to nourish "Us." We hopefully will have more time to create special moments and memories with those we love, to laugh over as our lives draw to a close. And at the end, we will pass into the next life holding the hand of someone who knows intimately the person we are and loves us unconditionally...for now and for eternity.

With that, we have come to the end of our journey together. Along the way, we have added stones to the foundation of your career, discussed behaviors to help you lean toward success and away from failure, and explored the roles that make up your life. What is next, you ask? To that question, I have no answer. Only you know that. You stand at the threshold of the most exciting point in your life when all things are possible, bound only by the limits of your imagination and the conviction of your spirit. However you choose to grow your career or live your life from this point forward, I wish you only the best.

Godspeed.

What Are Your Thoughts?

We want to hear from you! Tell us your thoughts about the book, your experiences as a new hire in the first year of your first job, or anything else you want to share. You can email us at **feedback@aspenmtnpublishing.com** or visit our website at **www.aspenmtnpublishing.com**.

About the Author

Once upon a time, Jason Smith was a new hire straight from campus, fumbling his way through his first real job. For the fourteen years since, he has held both corporate and field Human Resources positions in the oil and gas, merchant power, and media industries supporting clients in North America and around the world. Jason holds a Master's Degree in Human Resources from the University of South Carolina-Columbia, a Bachelor's Degree in Corporate Finance and Investments from East Tennessee State University in Johnson City, Tennessee, and a Senior Professional in Human Resources (SPHR) designation from the Society of Human Resource Management. He resides just north of Atlanta, Georgia, with his wife and daughter.

Printed in the United States
48189LVS00002B/451-471

9 780977 723768